insight text guide

Jenny McMillan

A Separation

Dir. Asghar Farhadi

insight™

First published in 2015, reprinted in 2015.

Insight Publications Pty Ltd
3/350 Charman Road
Cheltenham VIC 3192
Australia
Tel: +61 3 8571 4950
Fax: +61 3 8571 0257
Email: books@insightpublications.com.au

www.insightpublications.com.au

National Library of Australia Cataloguing-in-Publication entry:
McMillan, Jenny, author.
Director Asghar Farhadi's A separation / Jenny McMillan.
9781925134094 (paperback)
Insight text guide.
Includes bibliographical references.
For secondary school age.
Farhādī, Aṣghar, 1972—Separation.
Farhādī, Aṣghar, 1972—Criticism and interpretation.
A separation (Motion picture)
791.4372

Other ISBNs:
9781925175004 (digital)
9781925175332 (bundle: print + digital)

Cover design by Modern Art Production Group.

Printed in Australia.

contents

CHARACTER MAP

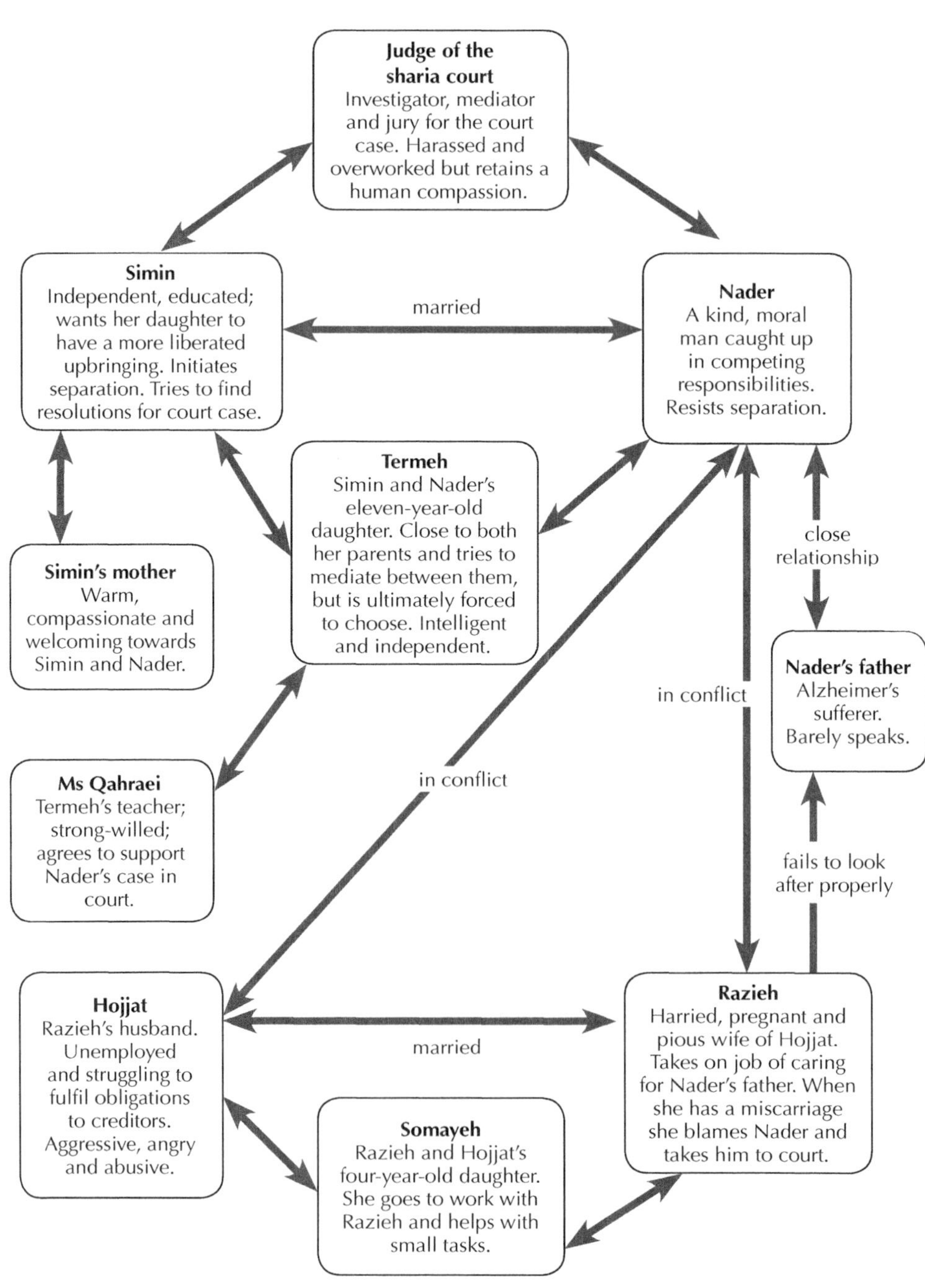

OVERVIEW

About the director/screenwriter

Cited in *Time* magazine in 2012 as one of the hundred most influential people in the world, Iranian Asghar Farhadi is the director and writer of *A Separation* (2011). After its release, this film was critically acclaimed as the best picture of the year in many international competitions. It won the Crystal Simorgh from the Fajr International Film Festival (Iran), and a Golden Bear and the Prize of the Ecumenical Jury at the Berlin International Film Festival (Germany). It was also awarded Best Foreign Language Film at the Golden Globe and Academy Awards ceremonies and by numerous American organisations including the Boston Society of Film Critics, the Chicago and Los Angeles Film Critics Association and the New York Film Critics Circle. In the UK, *A Separation* was nominated for a BAFTA Award for Best Writing, Screenplay Written Directly for the Screen. Farhadi was also the first Iranian film-maker to win an Oscar.

Farhadi, born in 1972 in the province of Isfahan in Iran, is trained and educated in Theatre. He holds both a Dramatic Arts degree from Tehran University and an MA in Stage Direction from the Tarbiat Modares University. He made a number of short films as a student for the Iranian Young Cinema Society and later completed two television series, one of which was *A Tale of a City*, for the Iranian Broadcasting Corporation. Farhadi acknowledges the influence of the stage, saying he feels more like a writer than a film-maker (Geist 2011).

Farhadi's films have won many awards at international film festivals. His first feature film, *Dancing in the Dust* (2003), won awards at Fajr and Moscow, while *The Beautiful City* (2004), about a youth imprisoned for murder, won awards at Warsaw and Moscow. His third film, *Fireworks Wednesday* (2006), which examined the trials of marriage, won the Gold Hugo at the Chicago International Film Festival. *About Elly* (2009), described by critics as a masterpiece, won the Silver Bear for Best Director at the 59th Berlin International Film Festival. *The Past* (2014), filmed in Paris, in French, is testimony to his talents for nuanced scripting, sensitive direction and finely layered drama.

The acknowledgement of *A Separation*, and by extension Iranian cinema more broadly, brought delight to Iranian audiences – or 'melting sugar to their hearts', as a Persian phrase goes. While the custodians of the Islamic Republic were doubtful about the Golden Globe award, Iranians around the world saw it as an instant measure of truth, differentiating those afflicted by politics from those liberated by art (Dabashi 2012).

Synopsis

A Separation unveils the complexities of judgement. The voice of the judge – mostly patient, tired of the eternal human struggle to make sense of life's confusion – suffuses the film, in particular the opening and closing sequences. There really is no simple answer in such situations, Farhadi suggests.

Set in modern-day Tehran, the drama of the film arises from the painful separation of a middle-class couple, Nader and Simin, and the consequences for their daughter, Termeh. After months of bureaucratic haggling, Simin, an independent professional, has managed to get a visa for her family to emigrate abroad. She wants to bring up her daughter in 'better circumstances' than those on offer in the Islamic state of Iran. But Nader, her husband, needs to care for his father who suffers from advanced Alzheimer's disease. Nader cannot leave; nor will he give Simin the permission she needs to leave with Termeh. Termeh, eleven years old, the child in the middle of the mayhem, then becomes the focus of judgement throughout the film.

The couple privately agree to separate and Termeh at first decides to remain with Nader in his modern, comfortable apartment while Simin returns to her mother's house. The family needs to find a carer for the grandfather so Nader hires Razieh, whom he barely knows, from a poorer part of the city. The arrangement seems unstable from the start, set as it is against Razieh's insistent haggling, complaints about the long commute, uncertain availability and exhaustion due to the fact that she is – as will soon be revealed and become significant – pregnant. She is also an observant, orthodox Shi'a who is not permitted to work either by her faith or by her husband. She doesn't mention her pregnancy to Nader, nor her job to her out-of-work husband.

The drama intensifies as Razieh, with her small daughter Somayeh in train, struggles to deal with Nader's father. Arguments with Nader escalate when he arrives home one day to find no Razieh and his father unconscious and tied to the bed. When Razieh finally returns to the house she doesn't say where she has been. The ensuing dispute with Razieh leads a furious Nader to push her out the door. She falls on the outside stairs and ends up in hospital miscarrying. It becomes apparent that she has been to see a gynaecologist after having been hit by a car the day before, while chasing Nader's father who escaped into the street. The miscarriage, for which her family blames Nader, becomes the subject of a murder case and leads to the demand for compensation, which is then reframed as a payment of blood money.

A complex moral dilemma is now set in place. There are issues of justice, class, differing religious views, conflicts in responsibilities within families, the death of a baby, the need for money; all these colour the truth of the case, intensifying the tension of the film. The court scenes, formal and informal, are suffused with half-truths and emotional manipulation. The tussles brilliantly unveil the fissures in Iranian society. The issue of truth remains always at the centre and all are guilty of compromising it.

The sharia court crowds the disputing parties into a small room where they conduct their argument in front of the judge. There are no lawyers; clients represent themselves while the judge acts as investigator, jury and mediator. If it can be proved that Nader knew Razieh was pregnant when he pushed her, he could be sent to prison for three years for murder. Blood money can be paid in the case of a murder plea.

As the case unfolds, Termeh becomes the detective and makes Nader acknowledge that he did know that Razieh was pregnant despite initially denying it. Razieh's husband, behaving erratically, stalks Termeh at her school and threatens her teacher. So Nader reluctantly agrees to a financial settlement, payment of the blood money, to end the case. The two families meet at Razieh's home but, before he will pay, Nader forces the religiously observant Razieh to swear on the Qur'an, witnessed by her family, that she believes his actions caused her to lose her baby. As she cannot do this, he does not pay.

The final judgement of the film, however, takes place in court with the divorce of Nader and Simin. The final arbitration – which parent to choose – is left to Termeh.

Character summaries

Simin

Simin is an educated, middle-class and strongly independent woman who believes Iran does not offer the best opportunities for her daughter. She works, but has shared the responsibility of caring for Nader's father, who trusts her. Her pragmatism and compassion make her a forthright foil to her husband.

Nader

A cool, educated, middle-class Iranian, Nader is an ethical individual and a compassionate father and son. He disagrees with Simin's choice to leave him and their country. He deals fairly with Razieh, his father's carer, but his class attitudes block his response to her dilemmas. With his daughter, Termeh, Nader can be playful but he also pushes her to think hard and to stand up for herself. He treats women with respect. For most of the film he is cool under fire and acts with honour. His ultimate acknowledgement to Termeh that he has compromised the truth, and his weeping as he washes his dying father, both reveal a deep humanity.

Termeh

Forced by her family situation to stand up for herself, Termeh is a central character. Her shy independence, curiosity and intelligence lead her to hold both parents to account. Faced with the awful choice of which parent to go with, she initially chooses her father, thinking this will bring her mother back. She rides the dramatic crisis of the film with integrity, tests her father's claims about the truth and, in the end, is both victim and hero.

Razieh

Hired to care for Nader's father while Nader is at work, Razieh comes from a poor area of Tehran and is oppressed not only by her feckless and violent husband but also by her religious orthodoxy. The need for money has led her to infringe religious rules. Pregnant women should not work; nor, more importantly, should they lie. Razieh is more inclined to haggle with the truth than to speak honestly – though at the end of the narrative she is compelled to reveal the truth.

Hojjat

Razieh's husband is in financial trouble with creditors who are at the door and even haul him away to jail. A hot-tempered man, he intimidates his wife and not only bullies Termeh and her teachers during the court case but also tries to bully the judge. He believes that he has been a victim of injustice based on his social class.

Somayeh

Hojjat and Razieh's four-year-old daughter accompanies her mother everywhere and tries to help her. Like Termeh, she watches and sees what is really happening. She asks questions and is plaintively childlike. The little white lace hijab she wears symbolises both innocence and the constraints beckoning in her future.

Ms Qahraei

Ms Qahraei is Termeh's tutor and also a family friend. When intimidated by Hojjat and phoned by Nader about the gynaecologist, she revises her deposition to the judge about Nader's innocence.

Nader's father

Nader's father is confused and suffering from Alzheimer's disease. Largely bedridden, unable to speak and in need of oxygen from a cylinder, he waits by the door for the morning paper. He has depended on Simin and the episode when he wets himself is connected with his distress at her absence.

BACKGROUND & CONTEXT

Historical context

In 1964 Iran established itself as an Islamic Republic based on the Shi'a sect of Islam. From 1980 to 1988, Iran was engaged in a long and bloody conflict with Iraq that left a war-ravaged country and an overwhelming social and political need for reconstruction. The post Iran–Iraq period was difficult and marked by governance shaped firmly around conservative Shi'a Muslim values. However, by 2010 the beginnings of political change were evident, in spite of Western sanctions, and an intermittent relaxation of moral codes came about, particularly with regard to cinema censorship.

Many Iranian historians argue that it was the burning of the Rex Cinema in Abadan in August 1978, when hundreds perished, that triggered the 1979 Iranian Revolution. This attack, by reactionaries who feared the influence of a particular film, demonstrates how Iranian cinema is of central significance to the Iranian people, dodging, as it must, the censorship of kings and clerics alike.

Cultural context: Iranian cinema

Amir Naderi's film *The Runner* (1985) was shot while Saddam Hussein was bombing Iran, and Bahram Beizai's *Bashu: The Little Stranger* (1986) was set in war-torn Iran. These films brought Iranian cinema global attention. Another Iranian, Jafar Panahi, who emerged as the film-maker of the post-Iran–Iraq-war emptiness and despair, is now serving a prison term and has been banned for twenty years from making films. In 2010, he defiantly released a film entitled *This Is Not a Film*. So Asghar Farhadi stands on the shoulders of a powerful and resilient film culture and joins generations of talented and courageous Iranian film directors.

Iranian film and its interpretation of its own society is gradually countering Hollywood-produced representations of Iran, such as *Not Without My Daughter* (1991) and *Argo* (2012). Events such as the fatwa (religious decree) against author Salman Rushdie (in 1989–98) and the US Embassy hostage crisis (1981) have shaped international perceptions of Iran, leaving a legacy difficult to shift. One of the driving desires of the resurgent and successful Iranian film culture is to open the eyes of the West to the true nature and complexity of the country.

Censorship

Iranian films are widely acclaimed for their creative power, despite the strict censorship imposed upon them. The authoritarian religious regime of the Islamic Republic restricts, for example, the depiction of relationships between men and women. All physical gestures of romantic love, including any touching, are forbidden. Women are barred from singing and dancing on screen; actresses are required to wear hijab – clothing that masks the figure and covers the hair – for indoor as well as outdoor scenes, even though this is not what happens in normal everyday life. Social issues considered volatile – for example, any attraction between the sexes outside of marriage – cannot be raised in a film. As a consequence, 'skirting the censorship codes' has become one of the most prized skills of Iranian film-makers, says Jamsheed Akrami (Recknagel 2014).

The hallmark of Iranian cinema, not surprisingly, has become its aesthetic of minimalism or omission. Subjects are tackled in indirect ways. By not showing something, you often reveal its existence more powerfully. The subject of adult romantic love, for example, can be approached through the eyes of innocent children. So in *A Separation*, we become aware of the disintegrating relationship of Simin and Nader through the eyes of Termeh.

To break the censorship code brings heavy punishment. Jafar Panahi, who won a Silver Bear at the Berlin Film Festival in 2006, is banned from making films in Iran for twenty years. He was arrested in 2010 and his jail sentence was suspended only after loud international protests. This shows that it is much easier to cooperate with the state. Once a script is approved, directors are provided with funding and some equipment. The completed film can then be shown in Iran. This is the path taken by Farhadi, who is unusually adept at minimalist cinema, although he claims that he would make his films the same way with or without the censors. His ability to win the approval of the Farabi Foundation (officially responsible for regulation) with *A Separation* is a wonder to many, given its subtle challenge to the moral authority of the state.

On receiving his Golden Globe award in 2012, Farhadi said that the recognition of his film allowed for a recognition of his country for its 'glorious culture, a rich and ancient culture that has been hidden under the heavy dust of politics' (Dabashi 2012).

Directorial style

Farhadi's theatre background informs his directorial style. After *A Separation* won the Golden Globe award, some critics claimed that Farhadi's directorial style was anti-cinematic. They argued the film was screenplay-driven or mired in the 'Bergman camp of "filmed theatre"' (Sicinski 2013). Farhadi's theatrical background, however, also helps him to explore the psychological drama at the film's heart.

Farhardi focuses on his actors 'becoming' their characters. Actor preparation, rehearsals from the start with a very detailed script, and the negotiation of words and actions between director and actors are all characteristic of this theatre practice. As the director, Farhadi also insists on knowing his cast very well, both as people and as actors. This is evidenced in the cast of *A Separation*. Both Peyman Moadi (Nader) and Shahab Hosseini (Hojjat) had already worked with Farhadi in *About Elly*. Sareh Bayat (Razieh) and Farhadi worked together on his 2006 television series. Sarina Farhadi, Asghar's daughter, plays Termeh.

Farhadi shot all the scenes on location except for those in the judge's office and in court, as this was disallowed. This choice sets up a documentary style, which draws the audience into a particularly close relationship with the unfolding events. It also means that the budget for the film was extremely low by Western standards.

Deliberate directorial choices that blur the edges of scenes, making invisible details important and leaving it up the audience to 'read' what is happening in the film, characterise Farhadi's style. This allows him to expose matters that could cause civil shock and displeasure. It also gives freedom to the audience and respects their intelligence. Farhadi has said that respecting the audience is always important to him.

The judicial system of Iran

In the sixteenth century, Iran adopted Shi'a Islam as its official religion and so, also, sharia law (Islamic law). This legal code is now integrated into an independent civil law legal system. The Minister of Justice heads the Supreme Court and there is a separately appointed head of the judiciary. All judges must be certified both in Islamic and Iranian law.

The courts of the Islamic Republic use an inquisitorial system. (In contrast, Australian courts are based on an adversarial system.) The Iranian judge considering the case is solely responsible for the verdict; there are no lawyers prosecuting and defending the case and no jury. If the case is serious, then two or more secondary judges will be appointed; however, the presiding judge holds absolute power.

Though sharia law is observed in the legal system, multiple aspects of it are modified. For example, the state has the ultimate say over the death penalty and the High Court will review death sentences passed by lower magistrates. Laws also allow circumstantial evidence to be used in deciding a case; this is permitted under the banner of 'the Judge's reasoning'. Long-term imprisonment has also replaced corporal punishments enacted as sentences in traditional sharia law.

Qisas, or the law of retribution, applies to a sharia class of crime involving personal injury. Where the injury was intentional, the victim or the victim's family is entitled to retribution – 'an eye for an eye', or a life for a life. But the victim's family can forgive the perpetrator of the crime, in which case the punishment is not carried out; instead the perpetrator must pay blood money, or *diyya*. If the death was intentional, then *qisas* can apply, but if it was unintentional *qisas* cannot apply. An unintentional murder would result in a legal penalty of a minimum of three years in prison. Sharia law decrees that the killing of an unborn child is murder.

GENRE, STRUCTURE & STYLE

Genre

A Separation is a psychological drama in the crime genre. The film commences and concludes in a courtroom where the invisible judge is behind the camera, therefore placing the audience in this position also. Given the inquisitorial nature of the Iranian court, this opening directorial strategy invites the audience into the film to be the judge. The narrative, a search for the truth, asks the viewer to decide who is right in the court case involving Nader and Razieh, as much as to judge the exasperated couples at the centre of the film. The challenge to the viewer, as the narrative unfolds, comes from the fact that information is often strategically withheld and so has to be retrieved or conjectured upon. Tension is created through these deliberately constructed uncertainties. For example, we are not sure what happens in the traffic when Razieh runs after Nader's father. Nor are we sure how much Nader has heard of the conversation about Razieh's pregnancy. Farhadi uses such blank spaces and narrative gaps to engage the viewer.

The film creates for the audience a sense of witnessing real-life events. For example, the camera captures half-completed conversations in lifts sliding up against hammered concrete walls, and strained contact between people inside cars, where communication occurs through glances in rear-vision mirrors. This gritty realism in the design invokes the crime genre. We are spared none of the court security procedures, the crowded shambles of the courtroom and its corridors, the exhaustion of the judge. All these details combine to create the dramatic atmosphere and to render any judgement more difficult and tense.

However, the film-maker's interest is in broad questions of judgement arising from divisions of class and gender and, in particular, problems involving people's understanding of themselves and of others.

There is no easy clue that reveals the 'truth', as sometimes occurs in legal dramas. Farhadi has said he is more interested in raising questions than answering them. The final courtroom shot, leaving Termeh to judge her parents, is an example: her judgement is not given. The final credits slide across images of her parents, divided by a glass wall, waiting outside the courtroom for this decision. The film may trace a criminal investigation but the overriding perspective is that judgement is never easy.

Structure

'Life can only be understood backwards; the trouble is, it has to be lived forwards', the philosopher Søren Kierkegaard said. Farhadi seems to have structured his film with this thought firmly in mind. His habit of cutting off the end of a scene places the viewer in the position of having to remember events, of attempting to surmise what probably happened. The framing of scenes almost always means that the viewer's perspective is a limited one, forcing us to consider what is outside and behind the scene. While viewers are watching a narrative moving forward in time, they are, simultaneously, always reflecting beyond the current scene.

Farhadi, essentially a storyteller, has constructed the larger narrative using a sheaf of interwoven stories. There is Nader's story with his now-helpless father and a daughter in crisis. There is Simin's story as she rolls her suitcase out the door, adding the CD she cannot leave, while at the same time leaving her daughter and her whole family. There is the story of Hojjat and Razieh in their crowded lodging, dogged by creditors. Against these 'household-in-trouble' stories are flashes of workplace stories: schools, banks, courtrooms, hospitals and, linking all these places, the story of the crowded streets and the dangerously weaving cars and those who journey across the city in them.

The film works with what can be described as a three-act structure:

- The set-up or Act One establishes that Simin is leaving Nader and so Nader is forced to employ Razieh to care for his father.

- The crisis or Act Two is initiated by Nader sacking Razieh because she has left his father tied to the bed. The crisis escalates with the loss of Razieh's baby and the spiral of arguing, intimidation and conflict which takes place in Nader's home, in the courtroom, in the hospital, on the streets and finally at Simin's school.
- The wrap-up or Act Three comes with Nader's seeming agreement to back down and pay the blood money. The meeting at Hojjat and Razieh's house furnishes the dramatic resolution to the action against Nader, but not the resolution of the film's larger moral dilemma. The final scene in court brings about the complete separation of Nader, Termeh and Simin. Its conclusion leaves everyone guessing.

The action appears to take place quickly over only a few weeks. The two couples come from opposite sides of the social divide; both their daughters are watchers and mediators. But the action brings these differing perspectives and characters together, firstly in Nader's middle-class apartment and later at Hojjat's house. The opening frame has Simin waving her visa in court, hoping for the family to leave the country together; the closing frame has the family in court and in pieces, but still in Iran. The film is thus strongly designed, shaped and patterned.

Style

Documentary style

The film shares some characteristics with documentary cinema. The director's role is de-emphasised and the story feels as though it unravels in a real world, resembling the way news reportage is shot. The camera-work seems to skim over details, simply capturing what takes place in front of the lens. Of course, this is not what is really going on in *A Separation*. The director is very much in control and the details captured by the camera, though they may appear coincidental, are all carefully framed and focused. For example, outside the courtroom Somayeh waits round-eyed on her bench in the corridor and stares at the shackles on a man's legs.

The camera focuses in close-up, first on the shackles then on Somayeh's white, lace-trimmed hijab. When it is later revealed that her father had already been in jail, the audience is invited to recall that shot of the anxious little girl in her snow-white hijab, contrasting symbolically with the shackles. The composition of the shots emphasises the contrasts between dark and light; threat and innocence.

Minimalism

Minimalism is Farhadi's preferred style. Even though censorship restrictions imposed by the 1996 'Code of Regulations' may encourage this style, it is a choice Farhadi has claimed he would make anyway. Invisible details can convey symbolism, and spaces need to be left in the narrative and imagery so that the audience can participate intellectually and emotionally in the theatrical experience: the film's minimalism creates audience engagement and psychological tension. Razieh's accident on the road, for example, is more hinted at than explained.

Similarly, it takes the audience's uncertain memory of where Nader was standing when Razieh was speaking to Ms Qahraei, along with Termeh's dogged inferential questioning of Nader, to show that he knew of the pregnancy. The camera leaves almost every scene before its natural end or sometimes omits events and interactions completely. The audience is compelled to infer the narrative details. How does Nader cope with his night in jail? What happens inside Hojjat's house after Nader and his family leave? What has happened to Nader's father at the end? Does he die, and what might this imply for Simin and Termeh? What does Termeh finally decide?

Framing

Farhadi frames many shots in *A Separation* by looking through glass that is frosted, fogged over or broken. This makes the world opaque and becomes a metaphor for displacement. Glass partitions, car rear-vision mirrors and wing mirrors, windows, glass doors and glasses are all used to separate and sometimes reflect. Balconies and stairwells are also used for framing, so that the viewer never sees all there is in a scene. This technique reminds the audience about the divisions and the partiality of the society. It demonstrates that something is always withheld, that nothing is black or white.

Delineations of space

Nader's house – with its many doors and private rooms and its security system requiring visitors such as Razieh to be buzzed in – is like a walled fortress, and is symbolic not only of class privilege but of the separation between people that class permits. Razieh's stretching for the key above the switchbox on her first day of work highlights how far beyond her reach Nader's world is.

In contrast to the modern architecture of Nader's house, and the bourgeois individualised space in which the family lives, Razieh and Hojjat's modest house offers open and public space. Couples, relatives and creditors all seat themselves around the main room and everyone present knows how to engage according to code and culture. However, though those in Nader's house seem separated, there is nevertheless a high degree of connection, as we see when Simin confronts Nader, face to face, over the kitchen table; while in Hojjat's house the sense of connection is an illusion based on lies and even desperation. Farhadi uses and subverts the settled Islamic conventions of public and private space.

Shot length

A Separation is constructed from short, multi-perspectival, sentence-length shots. The spaces in Nader's home and the spaces in Hojjat's home are conveyed in the same manner and with the same length of shot, in spite of one home being spacious and large, and the other cramped and small. Whether the camera is filming in homes, banks, hospitals or cars, the shot length remains constant. Through the joining together of the shifting scenes, the film's editing helps to communicate a distrust of fixed answers and an anxiety and curiosity fuelled by what cannot be seen or known: by what has been left out of the frame.

Children representing the audience

Children in the film serve to represent the position of the audience. They are the watchers and the judges. Young Somayeh, with her dark, serious eyes, is often shown silently and intensely observing the scene around her. Termeh, armed with her thinly framed glasses, listens in doorways, waits on the sidelines and eventually confronts and judges. She suffers her parents' separation most keenly and it is her logic and opinion that the audience is often expected to side with.

SCENE-BY-SCENE ANALYSIS

Section 1 (1:00)

Summary: *A husband and wife confront each other in a courtroom. Simin has a visa for the family to leave the country, but Nader refuses to go. He will not leave his sick father, nor will he permit his daughter to leave.*

The opening titles appear against the opaque glass of a photocopier, square on square, like a series of abstract paintings. The shunting carriage of the copier reveals and then hides a sequence of passports, a technique that achieves a number of things. Firstly, it establishes a rhythm that later shots will follow, echoing the pace of the copier; it is just slow enough for the viewer to read the individual details. Secondly, it leads seamlessly into the opening scene: the courtroom where we meet Simin, who has finally got hold of a visa to go abroad – no doubt involving much photocopying – and Nader, who refuses to go. This introduces the central problem of the film. Thirdly, the opening shots establish Farhadi's characteristic cinematic style. The shunting and clattering photocopier alternately hides and reveals the identities just as later scenes will hide and reveal aspects of character and plot.

The ensuing court scene mimics the photocopier's movement. Simin and Nader are static on their chairs, but shunting back and forth with arguments they have clearly had before. They sit still but their arguments, like the photocopier, mechanically duplicate. The judge before whom this is taking place is hidden behind the camera, so that the audience is directly addressed by the arguing couple and asked to solve their problem.

Simin is the protagonist of the film, driving the action. With her brilliantly coloured red hair, evident under her scarf, she declares her modernity. Her dispute with Nader is not about loss of love and respect; not yet. Their division is to do with Termeh and her future. Simin wants to go but Nader 'can give a thousand reasons for staying'. This matter about a future for women cannot be discussed in public but rather in the semi-intimate space of a courtroom. It is painful politically and painful psychologically.

Q In what sense is Simin and Nader's dispute a 'little problem'?

Q Simin says to the judge, 'I came here for you to solve my problem'. What solution would you offer? Why?

Section 2 (5:27)

Summary: *Simin moves out. The family realises how this separation is going to feel.*

The departure scene opens with the removalists' difficulty manipulating Simin's piano – which she has sold – down the stairs; the angles are tight and the piano-movers want more money. Then Simin's suitcase won't zip. Inside the house, the camera shifts from one stunned face to the next. There is Termeh's face watching through glass and around doorframes; there is Nader, pretending to cope but paying serious attention, shown through long shots that slide from room to room. No-one pays much attention to the new carer and her child, who also watch and wait. This marks a different kind of separation. Against the silent emotional storm of Simin's departure, Nader negotiates Razieh's job as carer for his father. He is curt and uninterested.

Nader's father senses what is happening. He is the only one physically hanging on to Simin. Simin is strong, but the close-up shot of her crying as she drives away shows her tension as well as her determination to make this move.

Q Close-up shots convey internal conflict strongly. Choose close-up shots of three characters in this scene and write short internal monologues that reveal each character's thoughts and feelings.

Section 3 (13:31)

Summary: *Razieh and Somayeh arrive at the house after Nader has left. In the kitchen they listen for the new baby. When Nader's father starts rattling the front door they realise he has wet himself. Razieh rings Simin first and then the Islamic help-line to find out what the rules about contact between men and women permit her to do in this situation.*

At the centre of this scene is Nader's father, distressed and confused. His uncharacteristic accident seems to result from the strangely hostile atmosphere he now senses. The new woman won't touch him. The cold distance she keeps replaces the warmth and compassion of Simin, for whom he repeatedly asks.

Meanwhile Razieh, constantly fiddling with her headscarf, seems consumed by anxiety. When the accident happens, she is frozen into inaction. Her apologetic phone call to the Imam, on what seems to be an Islamic help-line, dramatises her fear of sin. Islam forbids touching between unrelated men and women and the nervous, observant Razieh needs help to interpret the rule for this situation.

Some thirty minutes after Nader's father wets himself, Razieh, barricaded inside long pink plastic gloves, finally cleans him up, while Somayeh plays in his wheelchair. His helplessness and dependence do not seem to call forth much compassion from her. 'Get up', Razieh orders the old man, 'open your legs'. Razieh, in her pink plastic gloves, and her daughter, with her complicit sympathy – 'I won't tell dad' – seem to live under a fearful shadow of imminent judgement.

Q What are the Shi'a Islamic laws about touching between men and women? What do you think is their purpose?

Q How does the film evoke sympathy for each of the characters in this section?

Section 4 (20:00)

Summary: *Nader uses the experience of purchasing petrol to teach Simin to stand her ground. At home, Razieh asks Ms Qahraei, Termeh's tutor, for the phone number of a gynaecologist. In the kitchen Razieh tells Nader about his father's accident and tries to resign.*

Through the mirrors we see Nader watch Termeh as she fills the car with petrol. This is not a conventional woman's job and 'everyone's staring'. He is training her to be independent and stand up for herself, but she is shy and self-conscious. Her determined father then makes her go back and demand the change the attendant failed to return. Termeh is mortified but Nader is confident and insistent: this is an object lesson about a society in which women have to be assertive in order for their rights to be respected.

There is so much happening once Nader and Termeh arrive home that the audience is easily distracted from a key detail: did Nader hear the exchange between Ms Qahraei and Razieh about the pregnancy? The camera seems to be constantly pivoting through doorways on angles, moving from a sliding glance into the grandfather's room to a worrying linger on the oxygen cylinder and then back across the spacious comforts of the main room and into the kitchen. We see Nader's surprise (about his father's accident) from around a cupboard door, as he searches for tea.

In counterpoint (contrast) to the petrol station scene, Razieh, though working her headscarf around her face and scarcely daring to look at Nader directly, nonetheless lays out her complaints about the job boldly, requesting immediate payment. The final points of the dispute with Nader are made with the corner of her headscarf actually across her face and in her mouth. But despite her apparently deferential modesty, she knows she has the upper hand in the discussion. It is 4 pm – too late for Nader to find a replacement. So, having left Nader in the lurch, she returns, rings the doorbell and suggests that he hire her husband instead. Nader is forced into this compromise and, for her protection from her own husband, he must lie.

Q What differences between Razieh and the other characters are made evident in this scene?

Section 5 (25:41)

Summary: *Hojjat arrives late for his meeting with Nader at the bank. His lack of experience seems no impediment to his getting the job.*

Differences in social background are marked out when Nader – in a suit jacket, busy unlocking vaults in the bank, symbolically accessing money easily – meets Hojjat, who arrives for the interview in casual dress. With a glass wall to separate them and mark the class divide, Hojjat haggles with Nader about the inadequate salary.

The hasty interview, conducted in the middle of a business day, and involving a public exchange about Nader's father's toileting problem, mirrors Nader's distracted interview with Razieh. The extent of the class separation, articulated by the haggling about the pay rate, is evident in the financial desperation of the poor and their consequent exploitation. The interview itself reveals a lack of connection between the 'haves' and the 'have nots', and Nader's lack of thoroughness carries some irony given the job is that of caring for his own father.

Q In what other ways does this scene illustrate class differences?

Section 6 (27:00)

Summary: *Razieh arrives for work instead of Hojjat. While Razieh cleans, Nader's father escapes. Razieh, seeing him by the paper kiosk about to cross into the traffic, rushes after him. On the way home in the bus, Razieh nearly loses consciousness.*

The day starts with Nader hearing Termeh's vocabulary homework. Her teacher's incorrect version of the Persian for 'guarantee' must never be accepted, says Nader, even if it involves losing a mark. 'What's wrong is wrong, no matter who says what', he tells her. Nader's exacting standard for truth is questioned, even by Termeh, at this point.

Key point

Nader's refusal to compromise on the truth in this instance provides a strong contrast with his later behaviour when he begins to question his own truth.

Clad in pink gloves Razieh starts the day, not at her own home as she had hoped, but at Nader's. Her disaster story of her husband's abduction by his creditors does not seem to touch Nader. She turns to carpet cleaning, heaving the whole rug – which is much too heavy for her – into the bath. Somayeh, delegated to take out the rubbish, also finds her job too heavy for her and the plastic bag rips. Cleaning up distracts them both and the old man escapes down the street.

This key moment is shown through a montage of quick shots, hinting at the urgency of Razieh's search. The montage includes shots of Razieh running down the stairwell and along the street, her black chador swinging; Nader's father, advancing uncertainly into the traffic; and little Somayeh, on the balcony, watching things unfurl below. Before we see what finally happens, the montage ends abruptly, jumping forward in time. After the terrifying dodging in the traffic, the consequence of which is yet to be revealed, the whole family plays a game of table soccer. The game includes Somayeh, and the easy, playful scene belies the conflict to come.

Section 7 (33:10)

Summary: *Razieh and Somayeh arrive at Nader's house late the next day. Nader and Termeh come home to a locked house, Razieh gone and Nader's father unconscious on the floor. When Razieh does return, there is an argument and Nader pushes her out the door. She falls on the stairs.*

The central image in this section is the pitiful collapse of Nader's father on the floor, hands tied to the bed with Razieh's scarf, oxygen mask strapped like a blindfold across his face. Termeh finds him and her shocked sobbing fills the soundtrack. Her helpless grandfather has now become a prisoner in his own house.

Counterpointing this image of Nader's father is that of Razieh's distress, now obvious through her uncertain movements and pale face. The doctor's appointment set up through Ms Qahraei, the scene the day before in the traffic, and the fainting on the bus after work cumulatively remind us about her pregnancy. Tension built up through half-revealed details is used to dramatic effect here.

The crisis point of the scene is the conflict between Nader and Razieh. The more the adults move the children away from the argument, the more we are reminded of their listening presence. When Nader accuses Razieh of treating his father callously, she deflects with excuses, countering: 'He always naps at this time'. She offers no explanation for having left Nader's father alone and Nader's anger leads him to jump one step further. He accuses her of stealing. Razieh, furious, recognises his accusation as being based on class prejudice. Her dramatic shaking-out of her handbag as she leaves expresses her contempt for this unfair insult to her integrity.

All the shouting, apart from frightening the children, has brought out the neighbours so when Razieh falls on the stairs there are several witnesses to pick her up. Inside and alone, Nader washes his father and sobs. Distress is everywhere. Termeh's model house made for school that day, with its brightly coloured roof and jazzy outside umbrellas, perhaps signalling her dream of a life with greater freedoms and pleasures, lies abandoned in a corner.

Q Why does Razieh respond to Nader's accusations in the way she does?

Q What do you think Nader is feeling as he washes his father at the end of this scene?

Section 8 (44:33)

Summary: *Nader discovers that Razieh is in hospital. Simin and Nader visit the hospital and find that she has miscarried and her family is blaming Nader. Hojjat is angry and aggressive.*

The exchange of information between Nader and Simin is psychologically fraught. The camera again works oblique angles around doorways but this time the hampered viewing dramatises the tension between the separating couple because it highlights the fragmentation of their communication. Razieh's sister-in-law has telephoned Simin to abuse her. Simin and Nader have two separate versions of the story. Simin is weary of the conflict and focuses on assembling the salad, with only occasional glances and questions. The chopping symbolises something of Simin's state of mind about Nader. Trust between them is fraying.

The lift shot in the hospital tensely holds the audience's attention. A psychological revelation takes place as Nader and Simin are captured in mid-shot, backed by the sliding concrete wall behind the descending lift. The couple's stillness against the roughly textured concrete signals their doubt and distrust. They are, both physically and symbolically, descending to a very dark place.

The hospital scenario unravels the untruths about her employment and pregnancy that Razieh has been forced to tell the men to whom she is subservient. Hojjat's shock and wounded pride turn to aggression when he realises Razieh was working for Nader. Through the glass wall we watch the fight starting. Ironically Simin, the one who tries to stop Hojjat, is the one who is punched, but even this doesn't stop Hojjat, who is still shouting 'come out here', on the other side of the glass wall, as Nader and Simin leave.

Driving home in the car, Simin and Nader are very sober. The situation has become serious. With Simin nursing a black eye on Nader's account, he attempts, unsuccessfully, to persuade her to come back to him.

Q Simin has strengths that Nader lacks. What are they?

Section 9 (51:30)

Summary: *Nader is charged with murder. His defence is that he didn't know Razieh was pregnant and he counter-charges Razieh with neglecting his father.*

Reactions fired by class and religious differences intensify the animosity in the court. Nader's emotional self-containment sits coolly alongside Hojjat's increasingly insulting jibes – 'You trash', he shouts when Nader resists the idea of calling on Ms Qahraei as a witness. The camera, always in close-up, shifts from head to head. Razieh, often half-hidden behind Hojjat, is buried in side shot, keeping her own counsel. When Hojjat learns that Razieh had been employed by Nader, he turns on her furiously: 'I should sue you for working for a single man we don't even know'. Razieh, more distressed about the accusation of stealing, leaves the courtroom without even asking permission, her original intention in bringing the case now overwhelmed by more confronting matters. In all the mayhem, the long-suffering judge has yet to hear the whole story.

Razieh was four-and-a-half months pregnant, so the charge is murder. But concern about the loss of the baby and the grief of the mother is barely evident. Her husband's anger is fuelled by his conviction that this is yet another sign of injustice based on his class. The judge is harassed by too many cases and the intransigence (stubbornness) of the litigants. There is only Somayeh, outside alone amid the criminal world, who seems to feel the loss.

Back at home, Termeh and Simin hear Nader's phone message about being jailed. Termeh turns on her mother: 'If you hadn't left, Dad wouldn't be in jail'. For her the case is about her parents' separation. Everyone reads the case in the light of their own problems.

Q What would satisfy Hojjat as justice in this case? What would satisfy Razieh?

Section 10 (1:01:48)

Summary: *Simin posts bail. Ms Qahraei supports Nader's claim that he wasn't in the room when Razieh discussed her pregnancy. Hojjat insults the judge and only just escapes imprisonment. Termeh cross-examines Nader in the car.*

This section reveals the impossibility of the judge's task. 'I'll determine who's lying or not. You be quiet', he says at one point to Hojjat, who has been shouting him down now for two days. The judge asks Ms Qahraei to testify that Nader was not in the room at the time Razieh's pregnancy was discussed. But Hojjat is angrily dismissive. 'They fixed their story', he shouts, unwilling to accept any other opinion. The judge seems exhausted by all the noise and contradiction. He stands up to make himself more tea and get the window opened. On his desk is a line of empty glasses of tea, suggesting the repetitive, relentless nature of his work.

Hojjat asserts his religious belief as proof of his own truthfulness, and Nader's assumed lack of faith as proof of his untruthfulness. He then turns on the judge, educated both in civil law and religious law, and threatens him: 'You should fear God'. The judge has finally had enough. Hojjat escapes jail only through Razieh and Nader's pleas for mercy. The plastic sack containing Hojjat's antidepressants that Razieh waves in front of the judge testifies to his unsteady state of mind and encourages the audience to have some empathy for his situation.

As Nader drives home with Termeh, he undergoes a more searing interrogation than anything in court. He has trained her to reason, and his lie about not knowing of Razieh's pregnancy unravels under her pressure. What Termeh wants, though, is not so much his confession of the truth but his promise to ask Simin to return. He cannot do it. The section concludes with a strong image of Termeh, once home, sitting slumped with her grandfather on his bed: both in despair.

Q Hojjat says, 'The problem is, I can't talk like this guy'. What does he mean?

Section 11 (1:15:11)

Summary: *Evidence is gathered. Nader re-enacts 'pushing' Razieh. Razieh can't remember details of her fall. Termeh doubts her father. Somayeh reveals her mother was at the doctor's. Hojjat confronts Ms Qahraei about her evidence and stalks Termeh outside her school.*

This section opens in the kitchen, a recurring place for confrontations throughout the film. All the watchers are becoming doubtful. Termeh asks Nader if he is 'fixing his story' with the neighbours; his father watches helplessly from his room. Nader seems to be relying on evidence based on the mechanics of pushing and falling to prove that Razieh couldn't have fallen because of his push. In court, Razieh seems to be getting tangled in her lies. Hojjat is removed by force again. The situation is spiralling out of control. At home, when Somayeh cringes away from Nader as he hands her the colouring book, he begins to crack. She tells him where her mother was on that day. Things are now dangerous, particularly for the innocent: children, neighbours, teachers, parents.

The next evidence-gathering scene is with the doctor and Nader's father. It links with Somayeh's comment that her mother went to the doctor on that day and it dramatises this moment as a turning point for Nader. Nader starts unbuttoning his father's shirt but reflects, slows and then buttons it up again.

Key point

Maybe Nader sees the indignity to his father; maybe he sees that the accumulation of evidence is beside the point. Nader is now losing his certainty about himself.

Hojjat is gathering his own evidence and, with his wild anger and the Qur'an in hand, bails up Ms Qahraei at Termeh's school. His outrage is fed by Ms Qahraei's questioning of Somayeh about her drawings of her parents when she left the courtroom. 'You think we are animals', he shouts, 'I swear we're humans just like you'. As he is yet again escorted out of a public place, he shouts that he 'has nothing to lose'. To the horrified Simin he says, 'tell your husband not to make me do something crazy'. He seems to appoint himself judge, jury and executioner all in one. What he really wants is vengeance for the injustices he has been dealt.

Q List all the causes of this terrible situation that you can think of and rank them in order of significance.

Q How might an Australian court have proceeded with this case about a miscarriage?

Section 12 (1:23:46)

Summary: *Simin and Nader argue. Nader is cross-examined by Termeh and admits the truth.*

The scene at home opens with Nader leaving a phone message for Ms Qahraei. He wants the gynaecologist's phone number. Termeh overhears, realising that he must have known about Razieh's pregnancy. Next we are in the kitchen again, and Simin is smoking on the balcony. The camera varies the angles as the conversation between Nader and Simin heats up. Simin wants to arrange the blood money. Nader is furious; this is about his reputation and he will not admit guilt. Simin wants Nader to defuse the situation by paying, but Nader refuses, accusing her of being a coward as usual. She says, 'their child died'; he says, 'I won't be forced into paying' and that Termeh needs 'to learn not to be a coward like you'. The more they try to push Termeh out of the kitchen as they argue, the more the audience is aware of her listening on the other side of the glass doors.

Termeh, though, is no coward. She turns the next homework session into more questioning. 'Did you lie?' she asks sharply. So Nader admits he knew that Razieh was pregnant and that Simin was telling the truth. He tries to explain about knowing and yet not knowing when he pushed Razieh, but 'the law doesn't care about this. Either I knew or I didn't'.

This powerful scene dramatically reveals the truth behind Nader's posturings. He is actually less animated by principle and truth than he is by loss of honour. The accusation of cowardice he levels at Simin is both unfounded and unfair. It rebounds on him through Termeh's bitter question, 'did you lie?' She speaks the truth he dare not speak and he is forced to answer at last.

Section 13 (1:30:48)

Summary: *Hojjat is stalking Termeh at school, Ms Qahraei withdraws her testimony and the judge doubts Nader and questions Termeh.*

Nader is losing heart. First he discovers Hojjat lurking ominously at Termeh's school. Then Ms Qahraei refuses to communicate. Her withdrawal of testimony has made the judge doubt Nader and he also questions Termeh, who feels forced to lie.

For Farhadi, car interiors offer intimate theatre. Those sitting inside the car can be silent but their psychological turmoil can be communicated subtly in close-up shots. The heavy street traffic seems to reflect turbulent emotions between daughter and father. In this scene, Termeh, alone in the back, cries for her lost innocence. Nader's attention is divided between driving and witnessing the toxic repercussions of compromising the truth.

Section 14 (1:35:33)

Summary: *Simin negotiates with Hojjat about payment of blood money and attempts to persuade Nader to pay up. Termeh still hopes her parents will return to living together.*

Hojjat's exasperation drives his initial rejection of the blood money. He is edgy and upset while Simin is careful and conciliatory. By agreeing with him that Nader is to blame, she urges him to be 'realistic'. 'They're good people for giving you a solution', suggests one of the other men present, possibly one of Hojjat's creditors. Though Hojjat is in no position to reject such a large sum, he storms out of the meeting. He wants more than money. A man follows him off-camera, shouting, 'take a look at yourself'. The audience assumes that Hojjat has to give in; that he has no choice but to accept the blood money.

The scene shifts to Nader's house. The washing blows dry on the balcony. Simin sits in the empty house alone waiting anxiously for Termeh. Now she has taken decisions into her own hands. In the kitchen with Nader she tries to get him to sit and talk. But it's no use, the argument follows the pattern of the other kitchen arguments. Termeh listens near the door in defiance of them both. Nader will not compromise; he sees the blood money as bribing and extortion. Simin is frantic about Termeh's safety. The argument disintegrates around issues of money and Termeh's suffering, as well as which parent she really wants to be with.

Ugly compromises are being forced on everyone; there are no comfortable solutions. Nader withdraws defeated from the shouting and discord, and agrees to pay the blood money if Termeh thinks he is guilty. But now, finally, she leaves him alone and chooses her mother.

Q 'Take a look at yourself' shouts one of Nader's creditors. What aspects of himself might Hojjat need to examine at this point in the narrative?

Q Why is Nader forcing Termeh to be his judge?

Section 15 (1:43:39)

Summary: *Razieh and Somayeh visit Simin at her college to ask her not to pay the blood money; Razieh admits she was hit by a car the day before the miscarriage.*

'I have doubts' says Razieh to Simin, as she sits down at the desk, facing the other woman. So finally, the missing information is to be revealed. Razieh works her way uncertainly towards her revelation, confessing that she was 'hit by a car'. There is a long silence between the two women. Razieh's solution, that the offer of blood money be withdrawn, is no solution. It leaves everyone in the same legal and financial mess.

The long dramatic silence while the two women think about the consequences of this flawed solution is filled visually, as the camera focuses on the whiteboard and Somayeh's drawing of a large family. Most of her figures are smiling, in contrast to the people closest to her; seemingly, Somayeh, like Termeh, retains her faith in the possibility of family unity and happiness.

Q The final shot is a long shot through the classroom window, of Simin cleaning the board and putting on her headscarf. What deeper or metaphorical meanings do you think it suggests?

Section 16 (1:46:37)

Summary: *All meet at Razieh and Hojjat's house to hand over the blood money. When Nader asks Razieh to swear on the Qur'an that he caused her miscarriage, she cannot.*

Razieh is wrapped tightly inside her chador. She looks terrified as she gathers plates in the kitchen. Her husband, the creditors and Nader and Simin are all seated closely together in the little living room where a tray of tea is being passed around. Nader takes charge and breaks with protocol, asking for all the women and children to be present when he hands over the cheques. Razieh and Somayeh can't even find a seat in the room. Nader brandishes his money but first, he says, he has a request: 'Ma'am ... swear on the Qur'an that I caused your miscarriage'.

There is a search for a Qur'an while Razieh flees back to the kitchen. She cannot swear. Azam tries to persuade her to swear anyway; her husband thinks he can take on her sin. But she refuses. The presence of the creditors makes this final loss of reputation and honour especially painful. While Nader's family sit stunned in the living room, hysteria breaks out elsewhere. Hojjat storms out of his house and Razieh screams at Simin and Nader. The camera moves to the children's frightened faces. Then, as the film cuts to Nader's family approaching their car, the camera perspective is from inside the car window, showing their shock through the now smashed glass. Driving home, the splintered glass radiates shards of light as our gaze is held on the very serious Termeh.

Q What might Termeh be thinking as she is driven home in the car?

Q What do you think will happen to Hojjat and Razieh now?

Section 17 (1:52:2)

Summary: *Simin and Nader settle the divorce. Termeh is asked to decide with whom she will live.*

At the centre of this scene is Termeh's decision. Her parents have left it up to her to choose between them. The judge asks her several times if she has decided and she says 'yes'. But she wants her parents to leave the room before she speaks. She is testing a new solitude and new control over her life. The two parents sit outside, separated utterly now, a glass screen between them symbolising this. As they wait, the credits roll for a whole three minutes, accompanied by piano music. Other people make their way along the corridor; they have somewhere to go. Termeh does not come out of the courtroom. We are left to study her parents' faces. This is psychological devastation. This is what a separation means. We do not find out which parent she chooses.

Q Which of her parents do you think Termeh chooses and why?

CHARACTERS & RELATIONSHIPS

Simin

Key quotes

'Give me a reason to stay.'

'I came here for you to solve my problems.'

'How long do you want to keep this up? He's making threats.'

Simin: Learn what, fighting and obstinacy?
Nader: No, not to be a coward like you.

'Didn't you say it was my fault? I introduced you. If I hadn't left ... I have to accept it's my fault. Think of it as my dower money.'

'She chose you because she knows I won't go anywhere without her.'

Simin leaves Termeh and Nader, almost to make her point, that 'leaving' is something women have to do. Her absence from that household becomes a dramatic force brought into physical focus by Nader's father's dependency on her. The household seems to fall apart without Simin's guiding hand. Her strong reasoning and balance in the arguments with Nader show that these two usually argue respectfully. They may disagree about Termeh's future, but otherwise they share many values and beliefs.

Simin, a decisive, strong-minded character, is a realist or maybe even a pragmatist. She believes that waiting for things in Iran to improve is futile. Her daughter's future independence and freedom, she thinks, will only be found abroad. This justifies breaking up her home and her family. But acting on such a belief also requires optimism and courage. Simin's brightly coloured hair and casually tied scarf suggest a readiness for change, for what the West offers.

Key point

Simin has considerable power as the driving force of the action. Her creative life is expressed through her music (symbolised by the piano and the CD she takes with her when she moves out); she has a profession, outside interests and freedom to move. She goes where she likes in her own car. Her confidence commands respect and she is able to negotiate with men such as Hojjat and his relatives, as well as undertake the bail process, communicate with the school and deal with the bureaucracy that grants visas.

Simin's sharp eye for the truth makes her the first to spot Nader's lie about Razieh's pregnancy while also doubting Razieh's claim that Nader has been aggressive. We witness her principled approach when she advises Ms Qahraei to speak the truth when making her deposition. This approach, however, is put under pressure with the murder accusation and the subsequent threats to Termeh. Simin defies Nader and negotiates the blood money. She haggles with Hojjat, knowing he is under pressure from creditors. She is a pragmatist and eventually brings everyone to the table. It is arguable that she compromises herself when she leaves the family – including her grief-stricken daughter and her elderly father-in-law who depends on her. On the other hand, she is also compromised by the lies of others.

Her courage is a quality that seems evident to everyone but Nader, who accuses her of always running away. Simin believes that, in order to resolve problems, you have to stand up for yourself and then negotiate a practical solution. So she receives a black eye defending Nader when the fighting starts in the hospital. She keeps her word and stays silent, we assume, about Razieh's lie. She risks everything – her own family and future – for Termeh's future.

The dramatic contrast between Simin and Razieh, in terms of class, education, religion and employment, is one of the many separations the film explores. What unites them, and drives them both, is the need to protect their families while burdened by the restrictions under which they are placed as women living in Iranian society.

The 'why' of Simin and Nader's separation is not entirely obvious at the start of the film. It seems probable that they still care for and respect one another after fourteen years of marriage, but the 'little problem' noted by the judge is really a very big problem within their society. While Simin acknowledges over the course of the film that Nader can be trusted, that he is a good man, the fissures between them widen because their different attitudes represent different solutions to the politics of their society.

Nader

Key quotes

'When did I leave you?'

'How can I tell, I was away when she came ... always with the chador.'

'I won't be forced. It's extortion.'

'If you think I am guilty, go get your mum. We'll call them and go pay them.'

Nader exemplifies people who run into obstacles but still decide to tackle the problem. Such people are idealistic and choose to live their life based on principle.

Nader's refusal to leave the country is for more than one reason. He cannot leave his father yet he is being asked to choose between loyalty to his father and loyalty to his wife and daughter. He believes he must choose his father, because his father has no other choice. Simin and Termeh still have the choice of staying. Nader believes in his society. He thinks independent and strong-minded women exist within Iranian society: Simin herself is an example. So he tackles this problem in a forthright manner. We see him developing Termeh's confidence in the petrol station, in the court and through the homework sessions. He sets high expectations for her, even higher expectations than her teachers have. He also plays with her, trying to provide some fun in her life.

On the other hand, Nader's handling of the disaster with Razieh shows him in a less favourable light. He jumps to conclusions about her, saying this is what you expect 'of people like that'. From the start, he doubts Razieh's claim that he caused the miscarriage. But he did know she was pregnant and of course he could see she was religiously orthodox. All this should have made him extremely careful. But, at another level, he was not really 'seeing' Razieh at all. She belonged to another class. As the search for evidence becomes more intense and Hojjat threatens Termeh at school, Nader realises how very serious things have become. The fact that innocent others are gradually drawn in to lie on his behalf is a consequence of his own lie and this class 'blindness'.

To Nader's credit, he eventually sees what he is doing and stops. The turning point comes when he takes his father to the doctor to establish evidence about Razieh's treatment. As he unbuttons his father's shirt, Nader is overcome by emotion. His father is helpless, he has already been badly treated by Razieh and now he's being badly treated again. Nader abandons this project – uncertain that the bruising was from the fall – and does finally tell Termeh the truth. This shows the honesty he believes is essential to real relationships.

Key point

Nader is a character with whom audiences can empathise. His struggles to figure out how to work the washing machine or find the tea in the cupboards endear him to an audience, even if Termeh is slightly sardonic in her advice to him. His loyalty to and love for his father and Termeh and his juggling of multiple roles show he is every bit as compassionate and courageous as Simin.

Nader does salvage his honour in a way when Razieh's lie is exposed. But this is a highly compromised 'win' at the cost of a future for the woman who has just lost her baby. Nader's real separation from Simin quickly follows and here, Nader has everything to lose.

Termeh

Key quotes

'She is really leaving.'

Termeh: Everyone's staring.
Nader: Let them.

'If you hadn't left, Dad wouldn't be in jail.'

'Did you lie? How did you know Ms Qahraei had given her the telephone number?'

Termeh projects a seriousness and a wisdom well beyond her eleven years. Perhaps it is this stillness that focuses our attention on her as the suffering child at the centre of the divorce. Her pain, her need for both her parents and her persistent conjectures that her parents are going to somehow get together again counterpoint the cool rationality of her detective work.

Key point

Termeh's role as observer – framed through her glasses, which serve almost as a second lens for the camera – is intensified by her innocence. The decisions Simin and Nader make, their arguments, the negotiations for blood money, the terrible neglect of her grandfather – all affect her deeply but she can only watch.

Termeh stays with her father but is no housekeeper, dryly teasing him about how to work the washing machine and where to find the tea. Nor is she particularly obedient, insisting on listening through the glass when her parents argue and chastening them both for their broken promises. Beneath her reserve is a quiet strength and directness: a fierce independence of spirit. Though she is embarrassed and annoyed when her father forces her to argue with the petrol attendant, she does get the change they are owed. She has her parents' cool reason and their respect for the truth. She cries only rarely, suggesting her emotional strength and resilience, so when she does cry – for instance, when she finds her grandfather on the floor, or at the end, when she is forced to choose between her parents – the emotional impact is all the greater.

As the feminist symbol at the centre of the film, the one whose future we are concerned about, Termeh is one who observes and judges. In the end, no matter who she chooses, she still loses.

Razieh

Key quotes

'Will it count as a sin?'

'I lost my child but it didn't hurt as much as being called a thief.'

'I was hit by a car. My husband will kill me if he finds out I told you this.'

'Why did you come here tonight? Didn't I tell you not to come? Didn't I say we don't want your money? How will I live in this house?'

It might be expected that Razieh, shrouded in her chador and from the poorest part of the city, is the character with the least power, but in fact she fights her corner defiantly. She argues furiously with Nader about her dismissal, particularly about the unfair accusation of stealing. She confronts Hojjat's fury and the family's loss at the end when she refuses to swear on the Qur'an. Yet, despite her strength, she fears sin and its punishment more than anything. Razieh is, in a way, a moral contradiction. She is a religiously orthodox woman yet she seems to live a life based on lies.

Razieh's religious piety weighs heavily on her. Her pink plastic gloves, for example, symbolise a preoccupation with cleanliness linked to the religious laws. She won't touch Nader's father because he is a man to whom she is unrelated. So anxious is Razieh not to commit sin, she rings up a religious help-line to seek advice about cleaning him. To Western viewers, this seems extreme. So, the issue of cleaning and cleanliness becomes the trigger for the film's climax. As Razieh and Somayeh clean the house the day after his accident, the old man escapes. Razieh's religious orthodoxy is dramatised as an oppressive and fear-filled experience.

Razieh lies to protect herself and her family. She lies to her husband about the job because she just wants to help with the bills, and then she lies about the cause of the miscarriage. She does not tell Nader she is pregnant when she takes the job, nor about his father's escape and the accident. She lies to the court about the cause of the miscarriage to protect herself from the revelation of her other lies. In the end, though, she tells the truth. But neither her lies nor her truth protect her family.

The hopelessness of Razieh's situation resonates as the film ends. Everything she has done – her frantic efforts to live according to religious law, her struggle to help her inept husband, her confrontations with people who judge her and dominate her, her loving anticipation of the new baby – all this brings her to a situation even more terrible than the one she was in before.

Hojjat

Key quotes

'You should fear God!'

'I have nothing to lose!'

'The problem is, I can't talk like this guy.'

'Tell your husband not to make me do something crazy.'

'You think we are all animals. I swear we are humans just like you.'

Hojjat seems defined and confined by his violence and bad temper. He is an Iranian social stereotype of an unemployed working-class man and this, to an extent, explains Nader's muted response to Hojjat and Razieh's tragedy. Hojjat's bullying and intimidating behaviour reaches its climax when he tries to censure the judge for not fearing God and then bails up the teacher in her school. The full meaning of his having 'nothing to lose' is made apparent.

Hojjat has lost the capacity to support his family, as well as the respect gained from holding a skilled job. He has suffered the indignity of being jailed by creditors. He is infuriated in court, thinking that 'his type' cannot compete with the smooth confidence of those like Nader. In truth, he has lost respect for the institution of justice and he undertakes the gathering of evidence about Nader armed with the Qur'an. He is now fighting for his honour.

Through Hojjat's violence, Farhadi focuses our attention on class difference as a cause of helplessness and anger. We encounter a cornered man. Hojjat's wife is too frightened to tell him what is happening to her. His violent attack of Nader deflected onto Simin in the hospital courtyard; the shattered glass of Nader's car at the end of the film – such events tell the viewer that people who 'have nothing to lose' are dangerous to themselves as well as their society. They show the painful and destructive consequences of inequality.

The judges

'You are saying children living in this country don't have a future?'

'You can't file for divorce over every little problem.'

'I'll determine who's lying or not. You be quiet.'

The judges, both in the family court and the criminal court, are certainly not grandly dressed, nor are they ceremonially raised on platforms so as to preside in any physical sense of that term. In fact, their lack of support, their small rooms crowded with papers and glasses of tea and the necessity of sitting almost literally face to face with shouting litigants undermine the gravity of their work. Making judgements quickly and alone, while weighing up both legal and theological considerations, shows their weighty authority and responsibility – but in instances shown in this film it all seems too hard. Few judgements are made by them.

In the opening scene, there is only the judge and the couple in the room. Perhaps strangely to us, they expect him to step in and resolve their personal impasse. But he is exasperated and bridles at Simin's implication that Iranian society offers its children no future. This middle-class problem doesn't really rank in his view.

The even more harassed judge in the criminal court puts up with shouting and insults and with Razieh wandering out of the room. At one point he distractedly dips a cube of sugar into his tea, trying for some release from the madness. His initial confidence in Nader is rattled by changes to the tutor's deposition, and he is cautious with Termeh, too. He shows forbearance in the face of Hojjat's insulting manner but there is very little sense that the system he is part of can cope with its burden.

Parents

Nader's father can barely speak and his silence and mental confusion underline his helplessness. Though a suffering innocent, he becomes a catalyst for the crisis of Nader's marriage. His eagerness to read the newspaper speaks to a lost intelligence and lost civic engagement.

He suffers when Somayeh plays with his oxygen cylinder when it is attached. He suffers from Razieh's cold and distant manner when he wets himself, and later when she ties him to the bed before she goes to the doctor. He suffers silently when Nader takes him to the doctor to garner evidence. He cannot act, but he is acted upon constantly.

His escape bid when Razieh leaves the front door open is ironic since his life seems agonisingly inescapable. He is imprisoned in his mind, imprisoned in his room, tied up to the oxygen mask, and finally locked in his house.

Simin's mother runs her house and supports the larger family. She is supportive of Nader over the court case: 'shouldn't you tell us you're in trouble … so we can help you?' she pleads. Her wary attention and her physical and mental competence sets her in contrast to Nader's father. Farhadi has given the woman the stronger role.

Somayeh

Somayeh is a contrast to Termeh. Very young and already covered by the hijab, she walks in her mother's footsteps. She is curious and playful but housework is her destiny. She is prepared to hide things from her father, but determined to protect him, too. Her drawings serve as illustrations of aspects of her life about which she is too frightened to talk. Somayeh demonstrates Simin's point about futures for girls in this society.

Ms Qahraei

An educated, independent woman and a teacher, Ms Qahraei is gently professional and handles herself confidently whether with the judge or Hojjat. She is an intelligent and honest witness.

THEMES, IDEAS & VALUES

Justice and judgement

Key quotes

'You can't file for divorce over every little problem.'

'Get justice if you can.'

This film frames itself around the courts and indeed opens and closes in a court. Its camera work, mimicking a documentary style, seduces the audience into being the judge and attempting to decide what is right and what is wrong. But at every step of the narrative, with every shift in the perspective, the audience is confronted with uncertainty rather than clarity.

The very first judge we encounter refuses to make a conclusive judgement at all. He calls Simin's problem a 'little problem', but he – along with the audience who joins him in the perspective offered from behind the camera – realises that her desire to leave the country in order to obtain a just future for her child is no 'little problem'. The court certainly cannot decide this matter; it represents the state, which Simin has criticised as deeply unjust to women. In the end, it seems that there can be no just solution for Termeh's future at all. In the final court scene, Termeh is given the power to choose which parent she will go with but all we hear is her silence and all we see is her heartbroken tears. In this situation, both possible judgements are 'wrong' in that they bring negative outcomes.

The law seeks to judge right and wrong by applying principles and establishing rules based on custom. But these rules are incapable of responding to the subtle complexities of human relationships, especially in a theocratic society such as Iran's. The marital separation of Nader and Simin is caused not by mutual hatred but by differing views on how to live a morally just life. Simin's solution is to leave; Nader's solution is to stay. Nader is constrained by what he sees as just and right: his duty to his father. He does not agree that Iranian society is toxic for women. Both are concerned that Termeh should grow to her full potential, but their disagreement over how this future will come to be ends up in divorce. So, through seeking to provide more equality and justice for Termeh, they break her future apart. Being a parent and predicting the future involve judgements that are impossible to make.

The murder case against Nader concerns the death of an unborn baby, but this terrible loss seems barely registered by anyone involved. On an interpersonal level, the tragedy is immediately overwhelmed by Hojjat's violence in the hospital and by the spider's web of accusatory phone calls to Simin, rather than to Nader. There is nothing admirable about this violence and vengefulness. The injustice of people to each other makes the situation even worse.

The hustle of the court procedures, with the overworked judge who has barely the resources or the energy to properly assemble all the necessary facts, undermines any sense that justice either personal or systemic will occur. Our belief that the judge can rule on right and wrong is further eroded as the behaviour of a fractious Hojjat is forgiven. When the victim in the case, Razieh, mostly ignored by both judge and litigants, wanders out in the middle of proceedings, we lose hope. The court is at the mercy of all these human frailties: exasperation, exhaustion, violence, vengeance, prejudice and, of course, lies. The judge does not engage Razieh on the point of 'the blow' that caused the miscarriage; he is too preoccupied with managing Hojjat's anger and his own priorities. There can be no justice with lies, neither Razieh's nor Nader's.

Nader counter-sues Razieh for her treatment of his father in order to defend the murder charge. But how can the court justly weigh one injury against another; weigh an injury to a man at the end of his life against an injury to a baby yet to be born? That both injuries were to innocent and helpless people only makes the question of justice more agonising. Farhadi's harassed judge seems to have no rules, no ethical refinements, no energy and no time to bring to such judgements.

The gathering of evidence by Nader and Hojjat is very far from any notion of justice. In fact it descends to the level of farce, even though the characters themselves take it very seriously. The 'pushing' re-enactment outside Nader's apartment and the harassment of Termeh and her teacher under the banner of the Qur'an are both shocking parodies of justice. This escalating drama of threat and counter-threat has all the characters reduced to their lowest moral stature. So, Simin's solution of blood money seems pragmatic. The money, though, is a poor substitute for true justice. It involves a lie. Nader fights against this pragmatism requiring him to take responsibility for the baby's death. He insists on truth, but it seems that pride, more than truth, drives him. Everyone is compromised. Razieh, driven by her terror of sin, tells her truth to Simin. She refuses the blood money but would still let Nader go to jail through the court system. She would save her soul at the cost of another man's freedom.

The concept of blood money seems linked to a much older ethical social contract in which forgiveness of crime heals the damage crime creates. But the blood money in this film is no more than a legal accommodation that takes advantage of Razieh and Hojjat's poverty. How can forgiveness be possible when the grounds for the forgiveness are false? How can forgiveness be possible when the social separation between the two couples is so deep that compassion cannot flow? In the end, the blood money is not paid and there is, indeed, no forgiveness. Truth is elicited through tricking Razieh and using the Qur'an. This is very grubby justice. Her baby has died as a consequence of her trying to save the life of a very old and sick man. Moral reason might suggest that Nader does owe her, at the least, reparation for her loss and certainly much gratitude. The justice he wangles is therefore wholly compromised.

Key point

The shattered glass of Nader's windscreen and the shattered world he sees through this glass are metaphors for the broken social contract, the toxicity of class difference and the fragmented society around him.

Religion

Key quotes

> 'Will it count as a sin?'
>
> 'Ma'am ... swear on the Qur'an that I caused your miscarriage.'

For a Western audience, veiled women, with their veils swirling dramatically both inside the house and out, the black material like smoke across the screen, provide a motif and a metaphor of women's inequality and otherness in Iranian society. The veil encloses them, it even imprisons them; it hides their identity; it narrows them, clamping them all inside a particularised male gaze. The wrapping and unwrapping of the chador around Razieh challenges this metaphor. She uses the veiling to hide what she doesn't want seen: her pregnancy and her terror of sin.

At the heart of this religious code is the concept of sin. Religious law, like civil law in Iran, is based on rules and principles laid out in the Qur'an. Disobeying the law is a sin and the punishment for sin is dire. The Qur'an is borne aloft into battle, whether in the courtroom or in the classroom. Razieh's refusal to clean Nader's father and her phone call to the Imam; her attempt to reject the blood money; her insistence that Nader lie about her job to Hojjat: each of these events sets up a turning point in the film based on moral principle. All three also show how sin seems to hound and confuse Razieh. Rather than providing her with a clear path to living a good life, confusion in interpreting the moral law leads her to lie, to depend on guides for interpretation and then to fail in the simplest act of human compassion. One persistent image of Razieh, up to her elbows in her pink plastic gloves, conveys a person terrified of touching living flesh and obsessed with dirt and evil. The moral code, as she understands it, is about avoidance and fear. This moral code does not steer her to live a just life. In the end, her attempted adherence to her religion brings disaster to her whole family.

Farhadi's film counterpoints the religiously orthodox family of Razieh and Hojjat with the modern secular family of Simin and Nader, partly to show that both families are struggling to live in a principled way and both families in the end fail to live up to their own ideals. So it is ironic that, in the end, when the Qur'an is used as the moral enforcer, the audience sees a faithful, impoverished family manipulated by a richer family that pays lip service to this same Qur'an. More deeply, the audience sees how slippery the truth is; how implacable the rules.

The failure of these characters to live in a way that is consistent with their own moral standards and aspirations is as significant as the failure of the moral codes that guide them. Farhadi invites his audience to question Iranian society and any absolutist claims to truth.

In the West, religion has lost much of its traditional moral authority for the wider society, and many Western viewers may well have less sympathy for Razieh and Hojjat's religious commitments than an Iranian audience. Nevertheless, they certainly recognise the moral dilemmas of these characters, as well as those of Nader and Simin. The shock of losing a baby, the guilt involved in divorce, the responsibilities of caring for older parents and the terrible burden of divorce on children: these are morally and emotionally challenging situations that can face many individuals, regardless of religious background.

Truth

Key quotes

'If you think I am guilty, go get your mum. We'll call them and go pay them.'

'I lost my child but it didn't hurt as much as being called a thief. That's why I'm here today.'

For all that truth claims the high ground in this film, it comes with a very opaque quality. The shattered glass, the angled doorways, the enveloping chador, the used and abused Qur'ans: all remind the viewer that they can never see the whole picture. Testimonies tend to be revised when new facts emerge. Members of the audience, too, find their trust wavering. They realise, along with Termeh, that Nader, a declared champion of pure truth, is fudging the facts. His language becomes slippery. He pretends not to know that Razieh is pregnant, because no-one has directly told him this is the case, and – plausibly – the all-covering chador concealed her pregnancy from him.

Once Nader is charged with murder – an accusation he is sure is not truthful – he allows himself his own lie. He decides that the consequences for those to whom he has a duty outstrip the ideal of truth for its own sake. So he lies because he is faced with jail; he lies because he worries – who will look after Termeh and his father? He slides from idealism about truth to a truth system based on weighing and balancing consequences: an ethical and philosophical notion known as consequentialism.

There are no moral saints in *A Separation*. What feels to be right and wrong; what 'ought' to be; obligations and prerogatives: these are all constantly in negotiation with the mundane realities of life. Razieh, obsessed by sin yet steeped in lies, forces herself to tell the truth about the loss of her baby, but she does so for all the wrong reasons and still wants to conceal the truth. She lies and tells the truth to protect herself and her family. Nader lies and tells the truth for similar reasons.

Those who are imams, judges and doctors, burdened by work and with too little evidence to discern what actually is true, are, nonetheless, the arbiters of truth in this narrative. They are always men. Using the uncertain and constantly revised testimonies that come their way, they decide, holding the fates of others in their hands. But they are human too. In this film what does become clear is that there is nothing simple or easy about truth.

In fact, it seems that the closer we get to the truth, the more compromised it becomes. The actions of each character force the audience to face up to the heavy demands of truth and then to consider the cost – of surviving, of making exceptions for someone – and to consider whether duties to parents, husbands and children have a prior moral call. It is not so much the shortcomings of characters that stand out; it is the complexities of their moral judgements as they balance and weigh outcomes and inevitabilities.

Key point

Pure truth in this real world seems impossible. So the choices characters make do produce a tragedy of good versus good rather than of good versus evil. The characters are both blameworthy and blameless. There is no external, objective source of morality at all, it seems. This conclusion, in a film made in a theocracy, is indeed a conclusion to challenge fixed or preconceived beliefs and attitudes.

The role of women

Key quotes

'So the children living in this country don't have a future?'

'You don't have the right to do anything.'

'My husband will kill me if he finds out I told you this.'

The image of women in Iran, one constantly reinforced by the Western media, is of veiled women, kept passive, homebound and with very little legal freedom. This image is driven to a large extent by international feminist outrage at the inequalities enshrined in sharia law, which compels women legally to observe the Islamic dress code of the hijab, requires segregation of the sexes and encodes a number of significant inequalities in marriage, divorce and inheritance laws. But women in Iran have been actively agitating for a return of their rights since the establishment of the theocracy in 1979. They have had some success, as can be seen by Simin's capacity to request a divorce, to own and access money and to leave the country. On the other hand, there is Razieh. Here Farhadi shows a woman constrained by a husband who undertakes a traditional role as master. Farhadi leaves it up to the audience to evaluate the clashes brought about by the contrasts between these two different ways to conduct a life and a marriage.

The dilemma of equality for women is a central idea in the film, which opens with Simin looking directly at the camera (and therefore the audience) and asking for help with her problem. She believes Iranian society will poison her daughter's future so her only solution is to leave the country. But Simin cannot leave the country with Termeh unless her husband gives his permission. She does not have equal legal status in decisions that affect her marriage and her child. This opening focus is a bold move by Farhadi. His film, in Farsi, addresses itself in the first place to an Iranian audience, and if this audience is confronted by Simin's situation, surely the theocratic establishment will also regard this as a critique of the regime. The judge's ironic labelling of Simin's distress as 'a little problem' establishes the dilemma of the film. It is very clearly a 'big problem' and his judgement fails to recognise this.

Simin is a driving force in the film and highly active in society. She is educated, works, is independent, makes her own decisions, drives her own car and even extricates Nader from his threatening legal situation through the resort to blood money. Yet, in spite of this capacity to function deftly in her society, she has made the decision that her daughter can only have better opportunities if she leaves Iran. She has judged her society to be unfit for Termeh. This serious judgement costs her, in the end, and very dearly.

Dominating the film is the image of veiled women. To the Western eye, the hijab is a constant theatrical metaphor for enclosure and the implied male gaze. It frames women as objects of this gaze. It makes all women always accountable for the carnal thoughts they may arouse in men. Farhadi invokes the metaphorical power of the hijab as a screen or veil when Nader argues that it was impossible to tell whether Razieh, wearing the chador, was pregnant or not, even though she was working for him in his own house.

In Razieh, we find a woman who is confined by piety, pregnancy and poverty. The edicts that she must live by as a Muslim grind her into even more poverty and powerlessness. She must obey her husband, no matter how crazy and indigent he is; she must veil herself and avoid sin, even if she is unsure about its nature; she must keep herself untouched and clean. The only way she can evade the restrictions that impede her, and the way we measure her resistance to her oppression by her society, is through her willingness to tinker with the truth.

As a pregnant woman she should not be working, but she conceals this from Nader. Her deception exposes her to the real physical difficulty of managing Nader's father, her worry about sin and, in addition, her exhaustion from all the travelling. The image of Razieh, pregnant, chador flapping, running distractedly through the traffic, is hard to forget. The web of lies and deceit that follows this can largely be attributed to the terrible restrictions under which she has been placed as a woman.

Simin's initial question about the future for girls in Iran immediately focuses our attention on Termeh and Somayeh. We see Termeh being trained to stand up for herself, to think and study, to question her father ruthlessly. She is given the final say about her future. We can only speculate about what she will choose. But at least she does have a choice, while Somayeh has none. Covered already in the lacy white hijab, her future is framed by domesticity and subservience to men. She has also learned the necessity of lying. The two young girls show how fractured Iranian society is and how narrowly it can define roles for women.

Class

> 'I have nothing to lose. Tell your husband not to make me do something crazy.'
>
> 'That's what happens when you take people off the streets.'

Simmering explosively beneath the conflict of Nader and Hojjat is the divide of class. The divide, however, is about much more than just money.

Nader's comfortable apartment is far away from the cramped and crowded place where Razieh lives, yet she accepts the difficult job, the low pay, the gruelling travel and the likelihood that her husband will be angry, because she is desperate for money and in no position to argue. When the blood money is offered, the family is, again, in no position to argue. Fifteen million rial (about $1000) is a sum readily found by Nader, but represents for Hojjat the difference between sheer desperation and a real future. The divide in financial situations represents a lethal divide in social potential.

The class hierarchy gives power to those at the top. This is why Hojjat feels disempowered by the court process. 'The problem is', he says to the judge, 'I can't talk like this guy'. He believes he will not be taken seriously by the judge because he cannot act and speak as Nader can. Because he feels disempowered by class, he does not think he will receive justice. This contributes to his wild behaviour in the court when he threatens the judge – 'you should fear God' – and later when he pursues his evidence aggressively with the Qur'an as his shield. Hojjat's wounded honour is a danger to everyone. His notions of honour bind him up in a frightening charade of investigation, seeking his own justice because he has no confidence that the authorities will gain it for him. But maintaining honour in circumstances of poverty is a challenge. Hojjat is overwhelmed with helplessness, beaten down before the system. When he punches himself in the kitchen at the end we see a metaphor in action. What he says seems true; there is no other path left but madness.

Nader, on the other hand, presumes he will receive justice, but falls readily into class-based judgements of Razieh and Hojjat. 'What can you expect', he says, 'of people like that'. He doesn't question Razieh clearly to find out where she went, and adds fuel to the fire of class prejudice by accusing her of stealing his money. Unsurprisingly, his response to Razieh's tragedy is cooler than it should be. Given her strict moral standards, it is unsurprising that her response is to be more upset by his accusation of stealing money than by the loss of her baby.

Farhadi uses class to multiply the moral perspectives, demonstrating that different moral positions, even if mutually contradictory, can coexist. So it is possible for Nader to know that Razieh has lost her child while working for him but refuse to pay the blood money because his honour would be impugned. It is possible for Razieh not to explain that she was hit by a car, to undermine official court judgement by omitting this fact – effectively, telling a lie in court – and yet to refuse to swear a lie on the Qur'an. These positions show the normal daily confusions of judgement deepened by social inequality and resentments.

Family

Key quote

> 'If you hadn't left, Dad wouldn't be in jail.'

The intergenerational nature of families is at the centre of the film's values; *A Separation* suggests that wholeness, stability and continuity come through relinquishing and handing on experience from one generation to the next.

As children, Termeh and Somayeh owe duty and responsibility to their family first. So when Termeh is questioned she feels she has no choice but to lie to the judge about her father. Her tears come from clashing values and priorities and her focus is always on trying to bring her parents back together again. Somayeh shadows her pregnant mother through the day, helplessly watches the car accident from the balcony and even confronts Nader with the truth about her mother's absence. The most poignant family loss of all, the death of her unborn sister or brother, sits heavily on her heart. The scant grieving and the bitter drama of revenge that engulfs both families is Farhadi's comment about what seems to be morally lost.

Caring for family is one of the most persistent motifs in all Farhadi's films. The image of Nader's father being bathed comes at a turning point in *A Separation* when Nader finally breaks down and weeps. His tears register not only his outrage and his fear for his father; they also acknowledge his helplessness in the face of what has happened to his marriage. His household is falling apart, his cool confidence is shattered, and now he is a child again in his father's arms, while at the same time his father is like a child in his arms.

Key point

Farhadi here demonstrates that the identity and wellbeing of his characters are bound up with the roles and responsibilities they have within their families.

Simin's mother makes this same point when Nader is caught up in the courtroom disaster. 'Why didn't you let us know?' she asks, implying that there was never any question of their support. Simin's mother never stops mothering her. We see her in the background, anxiously listening as Nader and Simin talk about Razieh being in hospital. We are aware of her busy house, still full of people to look after. Her demeanour of unswerving loyalty shows how stability and responsibility make families strong.

Initially it seems that Simin and Nader's family is breaking apart because of the competing needs of children and parents. Nader refuses to leave his father. But he also refuses to accept that a choice must be made between Termeh and his father. He opts to stay and with this choice comes a commitment to a particular social and moral world. Simin opts to leave and with this choice comes a rejection of that world. She will take the risk of trying to bring up her child in the West, a different social world with which she has no apparent connection, and where one possibility – equality for women – outweighs all the other possibilities. So the family breakdown can also be seen as due to competing or conflicting values, to different choices that result from these values. It is no wonder Nader refuses to take the risk. The choice Simin makes is to put the value of the individual (individual rights, personal autonomy) above the value of human relationships (stability, continuity and familial ties). Farhadi's film weighs this choice deeply.

DIFFERENT INTERPRETATIONS

Different interpretations arise from different responses to a text. Over time, a text will give rise to a wide range of responses from its readers, who may come from various social or cultural groups and live in very different places and historical periods. Responses by critics and reviewers can be published in newspapers, journals and books, both online and in print. They can also be expressed in discussions among readers and audiences in the media, classrooms, book groups and so on.

While there is no single correct reading or interpretation of a text, it is important to understand that an interpretation is more than a personal opinion – it is the justification of a point of view on the text. To present an interpretation of a text based on your point of view, you must use a logical argument and support it with relevant evidence from the text.

Critical perspectives

A Separation directs its audiences to pause and reflect on universal issues, in particular the moral challenges involved in navigating the difficulties of family life and divorce. Critics including Peter Bradshaw of *The Guardian* in Australia, David Thomson of *New Republic* in the US and Rick Groen of *The Globe and Mail* in the UK write from the perspective of the film's ethical development and dramatisation of characters who are, at once, both 'blameworthy and blameless' (Groen 2012).

Some critics focus on ways in which the narrative casts a revealing light on issues of gender, class, justice and honour within Iranian society. Jason Solomons of *The Observer* (2011) comments on the way the film's 'creeping tension' pitches religion against economics through the issue of 'blood money', and so reveals fissures in Iranian society. The position of women in the Islamic Republic and the desire of middle-class women to leave Iran is the lens through which Andrew Macrae from *Metro Magazine* views the film.

Other critics draw attention to more universal themes and ideas explored in the film. Anthony Carew believes *A Separation,* like other Farhadi films, 'confronts viewers with unstable truths, questionable notions of justice' (Carew 2013). He comments that the film does this through metaphors of distance and division such as glass and door framing. AO Scott of *The New York Times* frames his review around the difficulties of being truly honest. Nader's is 'a house divided by exasperation', he says (Scott 2011).

Michael Sicinski from *Cinemascope* focuses on the psychological interiority of the film (Sicinski 2013). He reads the film as questioning whether we can ever overcome the basic human condition of 'separation'. Sicinski also wonders about Farhadi's seemingly free pass from Iranian political organisations such as the Farabi Foundation, pondering how he has tricked the 'cine-mullahs' of the Islamic Republic into allowing such a critical film to be made and shown in Iran: 'the censors are too stupid for words', he remarks wryly (Sicinski 2013).

A review by Nacim Pak-Shiraz looks at Iranian film from an insider's perspective, noting the subtle challenges in *A Separation* to the authority of the religious guardians of Iran. She says the film's key idea, 'the impossibility of attaining the truth', is a challenge by the director to the validity of the doctrine of 'Velayat-e-faqih' or guardianship of the jurist (Pak-Shiraz 2012). This power of the Supreme Leader to have the final say in the running of the country is now being challenged by many voices in Iran.

Two contrasting interpretations

Interpretation 1

In *A Separation* Farhadi argues that Termeh would have a better future abroad.

Though the judge of Nader and Simin's initial application is shocked when he hears Simin suggest that children might not have a future in their own country, the viewer comes strongly to agree with her. It is not merely the visual elements of the film – such as the recurring image of the veiled eleven-year-old girl – that support this view. It is the chilling separation of men and women; it is the bitter religious and social restrictions. When Termeh is given the chance to choose between her parents, we hope she chooses her mother and leaves Iran.

In their own society, the futures of Termeh, still so young, and Somayeh, even younger, are circumscribed and inscribed by the veil and its implication about a yet-to-be-developed sexuality. So Farhadi counterpoints the lacy white training veil of Somayeh with the swirling black chador of her mother. And as we watch Razieh, constantly pulling her chador over her head and across her breasts, drawing more rather than less attention to her hidden body, we see that her fears will eventually become her daughter's. Razieh is fearful of sin and fearful of her husband, leaving no room to openly negotiate her needs. The veil in this film therefore becomes a metaphor for imprisonment and distraction. So it seems that Termeh needs to unveil herself to be true to herself.

The separation motif in the film carries the image of veiling or screening into both public and private spaces. Communication between Nader and Simin is mediated or filtered by glass screens, doorways or balconies almost all the time. They actually never touch. This chilling separation stifles honest and intimate communication, and erupts into disaster with Razieh's traffic accident, and then the argument between Nader and Razieh. Termeh would be better off in a more psychologically open society.

But the religious restraints imposed on Razieh because she is a woman are the most damaging of all this society's limitations. She has to lie to her husband about working, so she is forced to lie to him about the miscarriage. This compels her lie to the judge. The Qur'an forces her to tell the truth. She not only loses the baby, she becomes responsible for the loss of all the blood money and so, it seems, the loss of family honour. Razieh, wrapped in her chador, symbolises the oppression of women brought about by her religion.

Termeh may not be as limited in her options as Razieh, but she is bound by the same religious code and by a culture that confines women to a secondary status. She must agree to a future husband's power, and she must remain veiled in public, perpetually reminded that her body is a sexual invitation to be averted. The film strongly argues that she must flee such a culture.

Interpretation 2

In *A Separation*, Farhadi argues that Termeh would not necessarily have a better future abroad.

At the height of the argument about blood money, Nader accuses Simin of lacking courage because she always chooses to 'run away'. He believes it is better for the whole family to stay in Tehran. It is a decision based on his belief in responsibility, duty and virtue. Nader's refusal to let Termeh go abroad fundamentally reflects his belief in his own culture. Nader is a loyalist. In taking responsibility for his father's care he is speaking for the principles of family culture. Simin, on the other hand, speaks as a pragmatist. She is prepared to break all her relationships apart in order to enable the social and political liberation of her daughter, Termeh. She puts all her trust in the promise of an open, tolerant Western society.

Simin is responsible for initiating the move abroad. But she is no coward, as Nader suggests. She is willing to deal with the courts; she fronts up to Hojjat and talks him into accepting the blood money, and then haggles for a reduction. This is a pragmatist at work. But Simin's solution is certainly not the solution Nader wants. He is concerned with his honour and with the truth. 'I won't be forced', he says. Simin characterises this attitude as egocentric and combative; as 'fighting and obstinacy'. Her arguments with Nader highlight not only the differences in their perspectives but two distinctly different value systems.

Nader is also a modern man and, though his marriage is ending, it has clearly been one based on respect and equality. 'When did I leave you?' Nader remonstrates, during the judge's questioning. He is a good man, he does not behave as though women are lesser beings and is as attentive as Simin to Termeh's independence. He wants Termeh to study, to stand up for herself, to be strong minded and honest. He meets Termeh's cross-examination of his own truth claim with more honesty than he shows the judge in court. In Nader's principled formation of his daughter, he shows his belief that women need education and strength to make their way successfully in Tehran. He pushes Termeh out of her comfort zone with his demand that she ask for her change at the petrol station and be accurate with her Persian translations. He weaves a sensitive line between giving her liberty and keeping her safe.

The society of Tehran may be mad with traffic and fraught with constant haggling, but it is Termeh's culture nonetheless. Nader is loyal to what he knows, even though it is not a perfect world. He won't risk Termeh's future in an unknown world that may bring some solutions but also some very probable losses.

QUESTIONS & ANSWERS

This section focuses on your own analytical writing on the text, and gives you strategies for producing high-quality responses in your coursework and exam essays.

Essay writing – an overview

An essay on a literary work is a formal and serious piece of writing that presents your point of view on the text, usually in response to a given topic. Your 'point of view' in an essay is your interpretation of the meaning of the text's language, structure, characters, situations and events, supported by detailed analysis of textual evidence.

Analyse – don't summarise

In your essays it is important to avoid simply summarising what happens in a text.

- A **summary** is a description or paraphrase (retelling in different words) of the characters and events. For example: 'Macbeth has a horrifying vision of a dagger dripping with blood before he goes to murder King Duncan.'
- An **analysis** is an explanation of the real meaning or significance that lies 'beneath' the text's words (and images, for a film). For example: 'Macbeth's vision of a bloody dagger shows how deeply uneasy he is about the violent act he is contemplating, and conveys his sense that supernatural forces are impelling him to act.'

A limited amount of summary is sometimes necessary to let your reader know which part of the text you wish to discuss. However, always keep this to a minimum and follow it immediately with your analysis of what this part of the text is really telling us.

Plan your essay

Carefully plan your essay so that you have a clear idea of what you are going to say. The plan ensures that your ideas flow logically, that your argument remains consistent and that you stay on the topic. An essay plan should be a list of **brief dot points** covering no more than half a page, including:

- your central argument or main contention – a concise statement of your overall response to the topic
- three or four dot points for each paragraph indicating the main idea and evidence/examples from the text. Note that in your essay you will need to *expand* on these points and *analyse* the evidence.

Structure your essay

An essay is a complete, self-contained piece of writing. It has a clear beginning (the introduction), middle (several body paragraphs) and end (the last paragraph or conclusion). It must also have a central argument that runs throughout, linking each paragraph to form a coherent whole. See examples of introductions and conclusions in the 'Analysing a sample topic' and 'Sample Answer' sections.

The introduction establishes your overall response to the topic. It includes your main contention and outlines the main evidence you will refer to in the course of the essay. Write your introduction *after* you have done a plan and *before* you write the rest of the essay.

The body paragraphs argue your case – they present evidence from the text and explain how this evidence supports your argument. Each body paragraph needs:

- a strong **topic sentence** (usually the first sentence) that states the main point being made in the paragraph
- **evidence** from the text, including some brief quotations
- **analysis** of the textual evidence, with **explanation** of its significance and how it supports your argument
- **links back to the topic** in one or more statements, usually towards the end of the paragraph.

Connect the body paragraphs so that your discussion flows smoothly. Use some linking words and phrases such as 'similarly' and 'on the other hand', though don't start every paragraph like this. Another strategy is to use a significant word from the last sentence of one paragraph in the first sentence of the next.

Use key terms from the topic – or synonyms for them – throughout, so the relevance of your discussion to the topic is always clear.

The conclusion ties everything together and finishes the essay. It includes strong statements that emphasise your central argument and provide a clear response to the topic.

Avoid simply restating the points made earlier in the essay – this will end on a very flat note and imply that you have run out of ideas and vocabulary. The conclusion should be a logical extension of what you have written, not just a repetition or summary of it. Writing an effective conclusion can be a challenge. Try using these tips:

- Start by linking back to the final sentence of the second-last paragraph – this helps your writing to flow, rather than leaping back to your main contention straight away.
- Use synonyms and expressions with equivalent meanings to vary your vocabulary. This allows you to reinforce your line of argument without being repetitive.
- When planning your essay, think of one or two broad statements or observations about the text's wider meaning. These should be related to the topic and your overall argument. Keep them for the conclusion, since they will give you something 'new' to say but still follow logically from your discussion. The introduction will be focused on the topic, but the conclusion can present a wider view of the text.

Essay topics

1. Farhadi has said, 'In all my films I touch upon justice … the justice of the system on people and the justice of people on themselves'. Where is the justice in *A Separation*?
2. 'Termeh is at the centre of the film as the wise child.' Do you agree?
3. 'In a society where women are oppressed, men cannot live in peace.' To what extent does *A Separation* support this claim?
4. How does Farhadi use the veiling of women in *A Separation* to dramatise the separations in Iranian society?
5. 'In *A Separation*, Farhadi shows that class distinctions are morally harmful to society.' Discuss.
6. "You should fear God", shouts Hojjat. How does *A Separation* portray the role of religion in Iranian society?
7. '*A Separation* is a film that exposes the slipperiness of the truth.' Discuss.
8. 'Every adult in *A Separation* is both blameworthy and blameless.' To what extent is this true?
9. Critic AO Scott describes *A Separation* as a film about 'a house divided by exasperation'. Do you agree with this view of the film?
10. 'The viewer feels that these characters will never be able to resolve conflict in their lives.' Do you agree?

Vocabulary for writing on *A Separation*

Blocking: In theatre, blocking is the precise movement and positioning of actors on stage in order to manage the performance fluently.
Chador: An outer garment to be worn in public. It is an open cloak covering head and body with no buttons or clasps, held closed with the hands.
Cinematography: The art or techniques used in film photography.
Framing device: A literary technique used to embed the surface narrative inside another layer or perspective. In *A Separation*, Farhadi uses glass and its physical/visual boundaries as a distancing layer of meaning, to remind the audience that they are viewing a perspective on the truth.

Hijab: In Arabic the term means literally 'screen or curtain'. It is a veil that covers the head and chest, and is worn by Muslim women beyond the age of puberty, in the presence of adult males outside their immediate family. It symbolises modesty, privacy and morality.

Imam: An Islamic leader of worship in a mosque.

Irony: A literary technique in which the surface meaning and the underlying meaning are not the same and may be opposites.

Minimalism: A style that simplifies design decisions around what is essential for the narrative.

Protagonist: The term refers to the main character driving events. Traditionally, the audience is expected to identify with the perspective of the protagonist.

Qur'an: The central religious text of Islam.

Shi'a: A sect of Islam formed after a dispute about the succession to The Prophet. The Shi'ites believed the leadership belonged to Muhammad's son-in-law, Ali. Shi'ites have traditions and practices distinct from Sunnis (another sect): notably their belief that the imams in Ali's direct line inherited Muhammad's prophetic spirit. Shi'ite spirituality has a strong focus on suffering and martyrdom.

Theocracy: A government or a state in which the political rulers are also religious leaders.

Analysing a sample topic

Farhadi has said, 'In all my films I touch upon justice ... the justice of the system on people and the justice of people on themselves'. Where is the justice in *A Separation*?

Quotations from or about the film provide a dramatic context for the question that follows. This quotation, from the director, focuses on an idea central to all his films, the idea of justice. The question that follows suggests that there is actually no justice at the end of *A Separation*. The quotation divides justice, a central theme of the film, into two categories: political justice and personal justice. The area the question covers is in fact very broad and you need to decide how you will narrow your focus.

Be very clear about the key term 'justice'. Frame a contention that answers the question 'where is the justice?' Is there any justice? If so, how much? Then make the important distinctions between 'personal' and 'political' justice and explain this difference in the context of *A Separation*. Decide what evidence you might choose for both kinds of justice. Then consider the techniques the director uses to frame the idea of justice.

- Find a key moment in the film when the most significant judgement is made. The ending of the film could work well. The justice being delivered then is both by the system and by the individual.
- Consider which 'systems' are in place to provide justice – for example, the court system. How is it presented? What seem to be its strengths and weaknesses? Weigh the role of the judge, his religious and legal background. Reflect on the evidence-gathering projects of Nader and Hojjat. Does this system deliver justice to people?
- Consider the 'blood money' system of restitution. Is it just?
- Consider the notion, 'justice of people on themselves'. Look at Nader first. Do his reactions to Hojjat and Razieh's accusation seem fair? Honest? Then Simin: is she right to leave Nader because he won't leave the country with her?
- What do you make of Razieh's notion of sin? This belongs to a religious understanding of judgement. How does this fit with her constant lying?
- How is justice for women shown as they negotiate attitudes to the role of women in the Islamic code?
- How is social justice raised as an issue, for instance by Hojjat when he confronts the judge and later when he is forced to accept financial restitution rather than the revenge he desires against class injustice.

The following response takes the view that there is very little justice in the film. Other responses might argue that Nader finally does receive justice when Razieh's lies are revealed, or that Termeh's right to choose which parent she wants to live with empowers her to shape her own future, therefore she receives justice.

Sample introduction

> The gentle 'touch' of justice at the end of this film is its most devastating moment. In inviting Termeh to choose between her parents, the judge is asking her to make a nearly impossible choice. As what she really wants is to keep her parents together, she simply remains silent and weeps. Courtroom scenes open and close the film but the world of the court seems inadequate to its task. Even more inadequate are the mock courts where litigants meddle with their witnesses. And worst of all is the mocking religious trial of poor Razieh, forced to swear on the Qur'an in her own house that she is telling the truth. Then again, the ethical standards that Nader and Simin set for themselves prove impossible to live by. In a society deeply fissured by inequities of class, religion and gender, justice proves to be provisional and compromised.

Body paragraph outline

Paragraph 1: The justice of the system collapses through both human and system inadequacies.

- The film is set up as belonging to the crime genre and positions the audience as judge from the beginning. Simin wants her problem solved by the judge, but faces the audience. The problem is personal: a family decision that threatens their separation.
- The court theme is reframed with Nader's murder charge. The judge cannot reach a conclusion because he is not in possession of the true facts; he is berated and obstructed by the class fury of Hojjat, and is exhausted by overwork and a system that requires him to be prosecutor, jury and judge.

Paragraph 2: Mock courts further degrade the pursuit of justice.

- The judge sends off litigants to gather evidence to support their claims. This involves mock courts on stairwells, in classrooms and on streets, e.g. Nader practises running out of the front door to test his theory, but he is not pregnant, exhausted or wrapped up in a chador and he does not have a small child he must hold on to.
- Think about the use of audiences to verify findings; staging and stage-managing techniques; *mise en scène*; repetition; religious authority in the form of the Qur'an; men's assumption of authority over women.
- The final mock court at Hojjat's house with the Qur'an elicits one truth but is not an example of justice. This couple has lost a baby, no-one really knows at what point; the family is poor and will be ruined financially and socially; no-one wins honour.
- Blood money is questionable as a system of justice because it depends on a monetary value being set on a life and, to be meaningful, it depends on genuine repentance.

Paragraph 3: The judgement of people on themselves is more focused and nuanced than the judgement of the system, yet still flawed.

- Sequences in the hospital lift and in the car use small private spaces to hold people closely together while they are emotionally distant and stand in judgement of each other, e.g. Simin's wary glance at Nader in the descending lift at the hospital – she knows he knew about Razieh's pregnancy; Termeh's tears in the back of the car after she is forced to lie; and Nader watching her in the rear-vision mirror, a moment of bitter self-judgement for him.
- In a reversal of roles, Termeh questions Nader about his knowledge of Razieh's pregnancy, using logical inference to unravel his claims of ignorance. Some scenes earlier, during a Persian homework session, he forces her to acknowledge that truth is more important than comfortable rationalising.
- Razieh, wrapped in her chador, lives in a complicated network of lies, yet relies on advice from others (judges we never meet) about how to be true to her religious principles. This ethical instruction

shapes her life, yet it fails to develop her moral integrity. She is unconcerned about the unjust nature of the court case against Nader, which results from her lies. The domination of her moral values by her religious beliefs limits her capacity for judgement, either of herself or of others.

Sample conclusion

The film's title, *A Separation*, speaks to the partiality of justice in Iran. The court's official processes are bedevilled by perceived inequities of class, the competing authority of the Qur'an and the dominance of a male world that barely stops to ask the female victim what really happened. The 'separation' of the film's title refers therefore, on a deeper level, to the society of Iran. The fissures created through differences of class, religious belief, gender and politics emerge in travesties of justice. In their judgements of themselves, people find that they cannot live up to ideals of truth and justice. The fact that this society resorts to blood money, the very existence of a parallel justice system of retribution, is symptomatic of the separations that erode and compromise justice.

SAMPLE ANSWER

'*A Separation* is a film that exposes the slipperiness of the truth.' Discuss.

With *A Separation* we seem to enter a zone of lies. The film invites its audience to puzzle out the truth, but from behind ever-shifting cinematic viewpoints. Typically, its scenes are cut off before their culmination, forcing the audience to trace events back and forth to try to assemble evidence about what actually happened. Even so, as director Farhadi intends, there remain more questions than answers. Part of the difficulty in finding a clear truth rests on the fact that the film offers no sure moral centre. The courts, making judgements that need to be based on truth, seem bogged down by overwork and an inquisitorial system that makes the gathering of evidence essentially untrustworthy. Religious truth, as declared in the Qur'an, seems anything but clear. Even the concept of sin seems clouded by obscurity and brings more confusion than certainty. Even those seeming idealists, Razieh and Nader, who claim the truth as their guide, ultimately fail to live by it. Everywhere, there is disastrous slippage from the truth as reality intrudes.

The two couples, separated by what they don't reveal to one another (a car accident, knowledge of pregnancy), illustrate the risky politics of lies inside a family. In many ways Nader is a morally strong character. He is tender and loyal with his father, respectful with Simin, and a principled guide for his distressed daughter. But his principles about truth, asserted so fiercely to Termeh when she is learning Persian vocabulary, come under stress as the murder trial builds up. He uses the chador as a reason for not knowing Razieh was pregnant. But this lie, believed by the judge but doubted by Simin from the beginning, is his undoing. Simin reads Nader like a book and is suspicious of his reaction in the hospital. Termeh, who has learned how to expose lies from Nader himself, confronts him after he tries to find out the gynaecologist's phone number. Nader's attempt to persuade Termeh that this lying is justified – because of the bad consequences for his family if he doesn't lie – fails Termeh's own moral test. For Termeh, Nader has slipped from his pedestal. It turns out that his lying is costly: Termeh feels compelled to lie herself to support her father. We imagine it may be even more costly for Nader, when Termeh finally chooses between her parents.

Razieh is morally admirable too. She faces challenging situations, trying to support her difficult husband and coping with grief at the loss of her baby. But in order to survive she surrounds herself with lies. Her religious principles, which demand truthfulness, and the fear of sin that holds them in place, seem to frame all of her behaviour. But truth slips away when fear and threat enter, and keeping lies consistent can be tricky. Moreover, when the blood money option is put on the table she finds herself in a religious bind. While she is almost casual about lying in court, she is very conflicted about accepting the blood money on the basis of a lie. Certainly she is not able to lie on the Qur'an. That Nader tricks the truth out of her, because of her religious belief, is a sad irony. And who knows the truth about when the miscarriage actually took place? Did it start after the accident, or did it start after the fall? Maybe both events contributed. In any event, the consequences, first of her lies and, even more, of her truth telling, are disastrous for the whole family.

Like the judge who oversees the murder inquiry, the audience becomes more and more dubious about the truth. The gathering of evidence, both by Nader and Hojjat, becomes very nasty. The mock courts on the stairwell with the neighbours, and in the school with the teachers, have more to do with manipulation of the truth (through intimidation, in Hojjat's case, or by the establishment of partial truth in Nader's case), than with the discovery of actual truth. The proposal of blood money as an alternative justice to that of the court is nothing other than a way out of the formalities and difficulties of the civil justice system. It seems, at best, a pragmatic solution and, at worst, a moral evasion on Simin's part. If she persuades Nader to plead guilty to the baby's murder, then they can pay the blood money as compensation and the matter will be closed. Hojjat is aware that his acceptance of blood money will deny him the vengeance he believes he truly deserves, but he is caught. His family needs the money. To Simin, who claims she values truth as much as Nader does, this half-truth is enough. So, in the end, Nader is offered a financial and a moral bargain to say he is guilty when he believes he is not. In the end he demands the truth from Razieh and exposes her lie. She pays. This is neither just nor moral, the film suggests, as the family walk back to the car.

Farhadi characteristically frames his perspectives through glass: either frosted, fogged-over or broken. This makes the world opaque and becomes a metaphor for the displacement of truth. Driving home from Hojjat's house through the traffic and in the rain, Nader's family view the streets through shattered glass. This is due to Hojjat's violence, of course, a sign of the bitterness of the class divide; but it is also a metaphor for Nader's shattered ideals.

Glass walls divide Simin and Nader as they await Termeh's decision in the court, just as glass doors divided Termeh from her parents' kitchen arguments. Even though she hears all they say she can't bring them together again. Now they must hear what she has to say but it will divide them from each other forever. We do not hear Termeh's decision about which is the better parent. That is the point. Farhadi wants the audience to make the final judgement and that is not at all easy.

REFERENCES & READING

Text

A Separation 2011, dir. Asghar Farhadi, Memento Films International. Starring Peyman Moadi, Leyla Hatami, Sarina Farhadi, Sareh Bayat.

Newspaper and journal articles

Bradshaw Peter 2011, '*A Separation* – Review', *The Guardian*, 1 July, http://www.theguardian.com/film/2011/jun/30/a-separation-review

Burke, Joseph 2011, 'Rediscovering Morality Through Asghar Farhadi's *A Separation*', http://sensesofcinema.com/2011/feature-articles/rediscovering-morality-through-ashgar-farhadi's-a-separation/

Carew, Anthony 2013, '(Di)visions: The Films of Asghar Farhadi', *Metro Magazine*, no. 178, pp.32–7.

Dabashi, Hamid 2012, 'Iranians and their Cinema: A Love Affair', Aljazeera, 5 March, http://www.aljazeera.com/indepth/opinion/2012/03/20123584823523724.html

Emani, Gazelle 2012, 'Asghar Farhadi, Golden Globe Winner for *A Separation*, Talks Getting Past the Censors in Iran', *Huffington Post*, 17 January, http://www.huffingtonpost.com/2012/01/17/asghar-farhadi-a-separation-iran-golden-globes_n_1209976.html

Geist, Dan 2011, '*A Separation*: At Sea in the City of Ten Million Tears', *Tehran Bureau*, 5 October, http://www.pbs.org/wgbh/pages/frontline/tehranbureau/2011/10/cinema-a-separation-at-sea-in-the-city-of-ten-million-tears.html

Godfrey, Nicholas 2014, 'Global Panorama: The Iranian Film Festival Australia and the OzAsia Festival 2013', *Metro Magazine*, no. 179, pp.58–60.

Groen, Rick 2012, '*A Separation*: A Criminal Investigation in which Nothing is Clear', *The Globe and Mail*, 20 January, http://www.theglobeandmail.com/arts/film/a-separation-a-criminal-investigation-in-which-nothing-is-clear/article630499/

Macrae, Andrew 2011, 'Miscarriage of Justice: *A Separation* and *Good Bye*', *Metro Magazine*, no. 170, pp.50–3.

Pak-Shiraz, Nacim 2012, 'Review: *A Separation*', *Ceasefire Magazine*, 4 April, http://ceasefiremagazine.co.uk/review-separation/

Recknagel, Charles 2014, 'Islamic Revolution Can't Upstage Iranian Cinema', 10 February, http://www.rferl.org/content/iran-islamic-censorship-cinema/25259188.html

Scott, AO 2011, 'A House Divided by Exasperation', *The New York Times*, 29 December, http://www.nytimes.com/2011/12/30/movies/a-separation-directed-by-asghar-farhadi-review.html?_r=0

Sicinski, Michael 2013, '*A Separation* (Ashgar Farhadi, Iran)', *Cinema Scope*, http://cinema-scope.com/currency/currency-a-separation-asghar-farhadi-iran/

Simon, Alissa 2011, 'Review: Nader and Simin, *A Separation*', *Variety*, 15 February, http://variety.com/2011/film/reviews/nader-and-simin-a-separation-1117944617/

Solomons, Jason 2011, '*A Separation* – Review', *The Observer*, 3 July, http://www.theguardian.com/film/2011/jul/03/a-separation-asghar-farhadi-review/

Thomson, David 2012, 'How Iran Produced the Best Film of 2011 – and What Americans Can Learn from It', *New Republic*, 7 February, http://www.newrepublic.com/article/film/100434/separation-iran-oscars-foreign-film-hatami-farhadi